Wakefield Press

KIN

Previous books in the series

Andrew Bovell: The Alchemy of Collaboration

Margaret & David: 5 Stars

KIN

AN EXTRAORDINARY AUSTRALIAN FILMMAKING FAMILY

including

Freda Glynn, AM, Warwick Thornton, Erica Glynn, Dylan River, Tanith Glynn-Maloney

with contributions from

Deborah Mailman, AM, Bruce Pascoe, Larissa Behrendt, Margaret Pomeranz, AM, Wayne Blair, Maryanne Redpath, Liam Egan, Faye Ginsburg, Mary-Ellen Mullane, von schtoop, David Stratton, AM, Bridget Ikin, Lisa Stefanoff, David Jowsey, David Tranter, Kim Williams, AM, Lee-Ann Tjunypa Buckskin, Scott Hicks, Steven McGregor, Philip Batty and Penny Smallacombe

edited by

Amanda Duthie

Wakefield Press
16 Rose Street
Mile End
South Australia 5031
www.wakefieldpress.com.au

First published 2018

Please note that images of deceased Indigenous people are contained within this book.

Edited by Anna Zagala, Sweetpolka, and Julia Beaven, Wakefield Press
Cover designed by Liz Nicholson, Wakefield Press
Text designed and typeset by Michael Deves, Wakefield Press

ISBN 978 1 74305 602 8

A catalogue record for this book is available from the National Library of Australia

Wakefield Press thanks Coriole Vineyards for continued support

contents

foreword

Sandra Sdraulig, AM

Chair, Adelaide Film Festival

The Don Dunstan Award was initiated by the Adelaide Film Festival in honour of the late Don Dunstan, Premier of South Australia from 1967 to 1968 and 1970 to 1979.

Dunstan's visionary commitment to the arts led to the establishment of various cultural organisations including the South Australian Film Corporation.

The Don Dunstan Award is presented by the Board of the Adelaide Film Festival in recognition of the outstanding contribution by individuals who, through their work, have significantly enriched Australian screen culture.

In 2018, the Adelaide Film Festival Board honours the extraordinary contribution made by a family of screen, arts and culture practitioners – Freda Glynn, Erica Glynn, Warwick Thornton, Tanith Glynn-Maloney and Dylan River.

From broadcast frontierswoman to award-winning directors, from cinematography to screen agency leader, across TV and film, the three generations of Freda Glynn's family have had an enormous influence on the screen storytelling in Australia.

Previous recipients:

2003 actor David Gulpilil

2005 documentary filmmaker Dennis O'Rourke

2007 writer/director Rolf de Heer

2009 producer Jan Chapman

2011 actor Judy Davis

2013 writer/director Scott Hicks

2015 writer Andrew Bovell

2017 critics David Stratton and Margaret Pomeranz

I would like to acknowledge the invaluable support of Arts South Australia who made this production possible. Thanks to CAAMA for granting permission to reproduce the wonderful Redback Graphix poster KIN, and to all the contributors for their words and images. Finally, I'd like to thank Wakefield Press for their ongoing commitment to the project.

biographies

Freda Glynn, AM

Freda Glynn was born at Woodgreen Station, north of Alice Springs in the Northern Territory, in 1939. Freda and her sister Rona spent their early childhood at the Bungalow, an institution for mixed-race Aboriginal Children in Alice Springs. Her mother Topsy stayed at the Bungalow with them, working as a laundress. After a period of displacement, Freda and her family returned to Alice Springs at the end of World War II.

Freda completed an associate diploma in Community Services from Adelaide University. This was the first program of its time to provide support for Indigenous students who hadn't completed high school so they could pursue further study.

Philip Batty with John Macumba, and later joined by Freda, founded the Central Australian Aboriginal Media Association Group of Companies (CAAMA) in 1980. CAAMA established Imparja, the first Aboriginal commercial television station, which commenced broadcasting in 1988 in Alice Springs, and was chaired by Freda for a time.

Freda's vision for CAAMA and Imparja was to deliver essential information and news to Indigenous communities in all the Central Australian Aboriginal languages. She was awarded the AM (Member of the Order of Australia) in 1991 for her services to broadcasting and to the Aboriginal community.

Freda retired in the early 1990s and moved to Cooktown in Far North Queensland. She continues to support her extended family and their various ventures.

Warwick Thornton

Warwick Thornton, a Kaytetye man, was raised, along with his four siblings, in Alice Springs by his mother, Freda Glynn. He gained work experience as a teenager at CAAMA as a DJ before picking up a camera, then trained as a cinematographer at AFTRS in Sydney.

Warwick is a director, screenwriter and cinematographer. Both his feature films, *Samson & Delilah* (2009) and *Sweet Country* (2017), have won a slew of national and international awards (including the Camera d'Or for *Samson & Delilah* at the 2009 Cannes Film Festival, and the Special Jury Prize at Venice Film Festival 2017 for *Sweet Country*), as have nearly a dozen short films. In addition to writing and directing, Warwick also shoots his own films and has worked as a cinematographer for film and television, across fiction and documentary.

(Photo: Mark Rogers, courtesy Bunya Productions)

Erica Glynn

Erica Glynn is a Kaytetye woman and was raised, along with four siblings, in Alice Springs by her mother Freda Glynn. Erica is a producer, director and writer across film and television. She has fostered Aboriginal filmmaking through her commissioning role at Screen Australia. In 2017 she was the recipient of the David and Joan Williams Documentary Fellowship.

Her films include the documentaries *In My Own Words* (2017), *Ngankarri* (2001), and the award-winning short film *My Bed Your Bed* (1998). In 2017 she wrote two episodes of the Aboriginal animation series *Little J and Big Cuz*. In 2018 she directed *She Who Must Be Loved* and *Truth Be Told: Lest We Forget*.

Dylan River

Director and cinematographer Dylan River is a Kaytetye man and Warwick Thornton's son. His debut documentary *Buckskin* (2013) won several national and international awards. In 2015, Dylan's first short film *Nulla Nulla* was selected as part of the Berlin International Film Festival. In 2018, Dylan directed *Finke: There and Back.* Along with his cousin Tanith Glynn-Maloney he is co-founder of Since1788 Productions, an independent Indigenous-owned production company. It allows them to make high-quality content across a range of genres and platforms.

(Photo: Tamara Dean)

Tanith Glynn-Maloney

Tanith Glynn-Maloney is a Kaytetye woman and producer from Alice Springs. She hails from a creative family and has always had a passion for Indigenous film.

Tanith began her career, like many Indigenous filmmakers including Warwick Thornton, Steven McGregor and Rachel Perkins, at CAAMA in Alice Springs. She produced *Nulla Nulla*, a short film that had its world premiere at the prestigious Berlin International Film Festival in 2015. The film went on to win the AACTA Award for best short film in the same year.

More recently Tanith produced *Truth Be Told: Lest*

We Forget with her aunt Erica Glynn. This one-hour documentary tells the story of Aboriginal men who fought in the Light Horse during the Sanai/Palestine campaign in World War I. Tanith is the producer of *She Who Must Be Loved*, a documentary directed by Erica Glynn about Freda Glynn.

Tanith and her cousin Dylan River are co-founders of Since1788 Productions, an independent production company committed to ensuring Indigenous stories are told through the Indigenous perspective.

(Photo: Dylan River)

Freda Glynn family tree

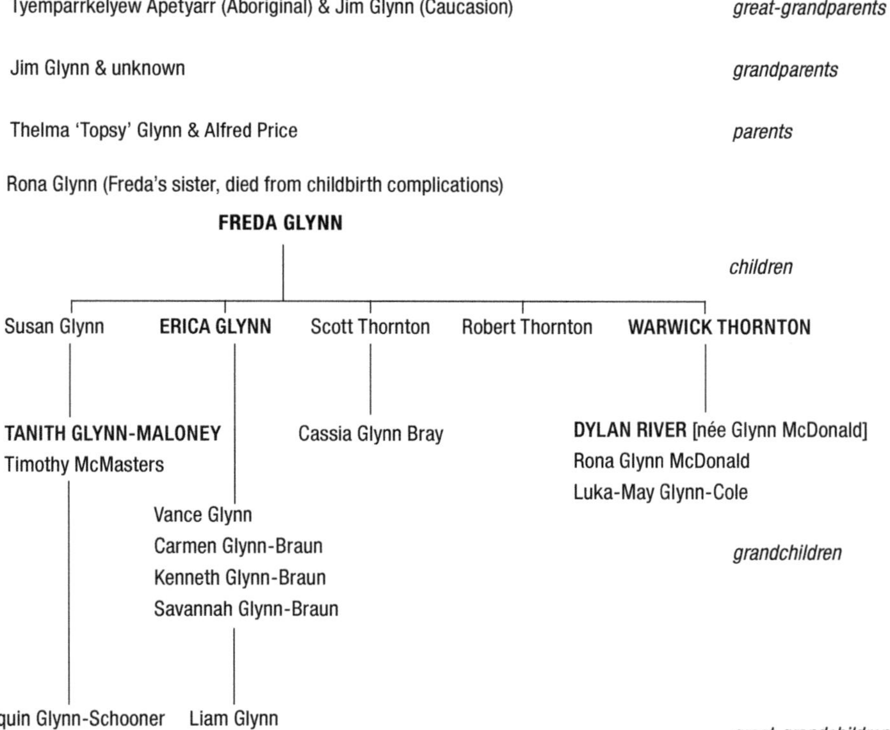

The multi-award-winning **Deborah Mailman, AM**, is one of Australia's most highly respected and celebrated actors. Her many film credits include *The Sapphires, Radiance, Bran Nue Dae, Rabbit Proof Fence* and, in television, *Offspring, Mabo, Redfern Now, The Secret Life of Us, Jack Irish, Cleverman* and *Mystery Road*. She is Bidjara (Western Qld) on her dad's side and Ngati Parou (North Island, New Zealand) on her mum's side.

introduction

Deb Mailman

How fitting, as we celebrate Screen Australia's 25 years of Indigenous Screen Stories, that we honour the contribution of this remarkable family.

Aunty Freda, Warwick, Erica, Dylan and Tanith are all outstanding in their own right, but what I love is that when they stand together as a family we get to see what they have given to our Australian screen industry, their extraordinary impact and legacy.

I haven't had the blessing of knowing Aunty Freda well but her dedication to establishing what is now CAAMA (Central Australian Aboriginal Media Association) has provided vital training and aspiration for Aboriginal people to maintain and sustain the culture and languages of Central Australia. It has also given rise to some of our most prolific and celebrated film artists, who have shaped the landscape with distinct voices.

Warwick was the first cinematographer to point a camera at me, along with CAAMA alumni Rachel Perkins, who directed me in my first feature film role in *Radiance.* We were babies in the industry's eye and now, some 20 years on, 'Wok' has made his voice known with a swag of beautiful and gut-punching films. He is an artist in the true sense of the word. Every time I hear that Wok is working on a new project I'm excited, knowing that he will craft it with great artistry and an uncompromising truth about what it means to be a blackfella in this country. Actors have their hands up wanting to work with him, and those who have worked with him continue to have their hands up, mine included. It's brilliant to be a participant in his films, and in the audience.

It's obvious what the influence has been for Warwick and Erica, how at ease they are with the filmmaking process, and what Aunty Freda and the CAAMA experience has passed on to the family. Erica has taken up the charge of continuing her mother's work with that rare combination of industry leader and artist. Her time at Screen Australia Indigenous Unit, along with Sally Riley, enabled wider community engagement to the screen sector, and brought a wave of Indigenous stories to life and the opportunity for a generation of artists to hone their craft. This dedication and advocacy to reclaim our narrative as First Nations people of this country has seen, in the last few decades, a spectacular birth of films, documentaries, television drama and comedy that has well and truly put us on the map. More importantly, we get to tell our stories in the way we want to tell them, and Erica has been instrumental in facilitating this.

But let's not forget she is an artist. I've had the pleasure of working with Erica and it bloody floors me how she works. She brings a visceral and intellectual lens to any creative process and just like Wok, slam dunks it with great craft and honesty. And now the baton has been passed onto Dylan and Tanith who are making their own strides in the industry. There must be something in that red desert soil.

Thank you to the Glynn family for all that you have given and continue to give. You are trailblazers and I know that my work is only possible because of everything you have achieved for us mob.

Bruce Pascoe is a Yuin, Bunurong, Tasmanian man. He is a prolific writer of fiction and non-fiction including *Night Animals, Fox, Ruby Eyed Coucal, Shark, Ocean, Earth, Bloke, Cape Otway, Convincing Ground, Little Red Yellow and Black Book, Fog a Dox* and *Dark Emu.* He has won numerous literary awards, most recently the 2016 NSW Premier's Award and, in 2018, the Australia Council's Lifetime Achievement Award.

Freda's fingerprints

Bruce Pascoe

Twenty years ago I tuned in to a film already in progress and became engrossed. I felt I knew the community. Even the layout of the building looked familiar, the people. I'd seen that hat, that face, that rascal dog. The whole thing was eerily familiar and real.

I found I'd been watching *Green Bush*. I looked for the director's name and discovered it was a Thornton. I loved that film and the casual love it displayed, the humour in the difficult community situation. It felt like a miniature masterpiece. Young Warwick, eh. Watch out!

When Film Australia wanted to fast track more Aboriginal and Torres Strait Islander filmmakers it was Erica Glynn who found the people and cleared the way for their training, the nurturing and support. She nursed my first film, *Black Chook*, through all the development and production phases, and I valued the fact that an Aboriginal person was doing it and showing such refreshing common sense. I was green and needed that confident low-key approach.

Recently I sat next to one of my big tough brother filmmakers as we watched Erica's language film, *In Their Own Words*. He was sobbing by the end of it, floored by the poignancy of old people learning to recognise and spell 'dog'. 'Could have been my uncle,' he said, 'my aunt, any of our mob.' And many of mine. Most of my friends don't read books, bemused by my writing, what I call an occupation. Some don't read books because they can't. It's a horrible affliction and, like starvation, an indictment of a wealthy country.

Erica's film brought us to the coalface of Aboriginal dispossession. We watched real Aboriginal people fighting massive disadvantage with modest heroism, a truly great documentary and a great lesson for the country. And of course it was brought to us by a Glynn.

When *Black Chook* came to production I was introduced to Warwick's son, Dylan River. I watched the no-fuss application of his vision and the tact he employed with everyone on the set. Having a writer on set is not what directors want, so they marginalised me, neutralised me, made me an extra. A non-speaking part. Out of the way. In one scene Warwick was shooting over my shoulder as he and Dylan were organising the direction. I learnt more about film and art in those few hours than at any other time. The discrimination, the innate sense of style. I loved that discussion. And they loved it because I couldn't talk back.

Freda Glynn was on that set too. Worrying about lines, stoic in her waiting as scene rolled into scene. I have a vivid memory of Freda and Jack Charles sitting against a corrugated-iron wall so lit by the sun that it looked like a spaghetti western. The two murmured to each other as they waited, all wardrobed, made up, waiting while a scene was organised. Professionals, seasoned waiters.

The whole film was a Glynn family event and for me the concentration of learning was intense. Working with Jack Charles, too, has always been a pleasure. Jack is convinced we're related but I had to point out to him that white beards in themselves are not a genetic marker.

Later I worked with Warwick on *We Don't Need a Map*, a bizarre experience in an art deco-ish house in Sydney's southern beaches. I didn't know what I was there for so just did the lizard trick, waiting and watching. Watched Warwick, how he went about his business, knowing he was fearless in going to the heart of Australia's ignorance of its history. I was right, he pinned every dead butterfly of Australian cartoon history to the wall. We had a great time.

At smoko I snuck a glance at Warwick's script, more shopping list or scatological memoir than script, but you could see the bones of his refusal to let Australia off the hook. He's a freak the way he makes films. Film educators look away now!

The whole family is a freak. Imagine Freda setting up CAAMA in an era where paternalism was still morphing out of disdain, where our pillow was still being smoothed for our passing. Imagine doing that black. Imagine doing that as a black woman. A poor black woman.

Some contributions to the country's history are so massive it is as if they are monoliths of country. CAAMA is one of those monoliths, its existence a testament to implacable defiance, its monolith bringing a black voice to a black land.

I was in Alice Springs doing some post-production shots for Trisha Morton-Thomas's *Occupation Native*, and it was Dylan who rocked up to film it, his ute already packed so he could smash across the desert to film the Finke River Race. He and Warwick are addicts to this annual off-road motorsport event, and have the broken bones and destroyed vehicles to prove it. This time they were filming it and Dylan was all jittery excitement at the prospect of riding like a lens cowboy in a chopper while careering over sand dunes and cars screaming like hornets.

I think motorbike racing is as pleasant as killing horses but those lads love it and in a weird way it is because it's an event on their country, that in this age for all its troubles they can take part in an event on *their* country on *their* terms. Justice can arrive unexpectedly, like the toy in a Kinder Surprise.

Australia, the only country in the world not to have made a treaty with the Indigenous people they dispossessed, holds steadfastly to a history so ridiculous in its conception that Europeans laugh in grim mirth at its profound blindness. The real history of the country was eliminated from our curriculum, our society, our politics, our morality. If the best-educated people in the land, the mild professors and urbane historians, can fabricate a history of such blinding connivance then another tactic has to be employed if the oppressed are to receive any form of justice. And that new tactic is an old one: story.

Story as painting, story as sport, story as dance and music, and now, most potently, story as film. Freda's mob have used the silver screen as a Trojan horse, where in the dark of the cinema, black soldiers creep from acceptable sculpture and lay siege to your city. It is insurrection, it is insouciance, and they're fucking good at it.

Warwick has done it with *Sweet Country*, using the form beloved of white cinema, the Western, the American folkloric way of explaining away the dispossession of the injuns. He slides the cowboy carpet out from under comfortable feet and turns it into a political statement. It is magic, it is a guerrilla war tactic, it is how countries get ambushed, forced to come face to face with history or the fake dynamite blows up and kills their faithful dog. Hooley dooley.

Dylan did it in his documentary on young Kaurna man, Jack Buckskin, the sole teacher of his language. Just another doco of a determined young teacher in some ways, but Buckskin is so softly spoken, so eloquent, that his message creeps up on the audience. Aboriginal language? Most Australians, if they think of Aborigines speaking at all, think there is only one language, so the information that there are many is a little bit of insurrection. Buckskin's soft voice, River's gentle camera, the iron fist in the velvet glove.

Erica did it with her language film. Just a mob of blacks

struggling with their education, or is there a subtle, sneaking message here that education deprivation is a colonial tool, treat 'em like mushrooms; keep 'em in the dark and eating shit.

You can intervene in your own fate, the fate assumed for you by those who have designated your position on the social ladder as sub-human, and therefore slave. When Freda began her decades long campaign to give Aboriginal people a voice it was an act of resistance, a refusal to accept her fate.

The resistance has been maintained by the whole family. In Warwick's film, *Samson & Delilah*, Scott Thornton as Gonzo gives one of the most poignant performances ever seen on Australian screens. Pain and trouble seep from him and highlight the uphill battle of the two younger characters. Warwick also shot *The Sapphires*, a film at the other end of the entertainment spectrum; like *The Castle* it made Australians feel more comfortable with themselves.

Both Warwick and Erica were involved with the series *Redfern Now*, a moment in the country's history that demonstrated a shift in psyche. Black, black, black entertainment – and shown on prime-time Australian television. You couldn't imagine such a thing only a few years before.

You can see Freda's fingerprints all over that achievement because she broke the glass, sand and colour ceiling to allow an easier ride for all those who followed, she created an expectation that Aboriginal people could compete in white media and cultural forms.

So from no say in the media a situation is created where Aboriginal people can talk to mainstream Australia about history, our shared history. As Warwick said of his own films, 'They're dark, but they're completely truthful.' Australia needs that truth. It may not know that yet but when it does it will realise a substantial part of that truth was delivered to them by one family.

Dr Philip Batty

co-founded and jointly managed the Central Australian Aboriginal Media Association from 1980–1990, becoming CEO of the National Aboriginal Cultural Institute in 1991. He has published widely, produced television documentaries and exhibitions, and was the recipient of numerous awards including the UNESCO McLuhan-Teleglobe Media Award. After completing a PhD he was appointed senior curator, Melbourne Museum.

Freda Glynn and the evolution of CAAMA: a personal reflection

Philip Batty

Throughout the 1980s, Freda Glynn and I worked together on the development of the Central Australian Aboriginal Media Association (CAAMA), now considered to be a cultural icon of national significance. Under our joint management, CAAMA launched the first Aboriginal-owned radio broadcasting network in Australia (8KIN-FM); founded the first Aboriginal video production company (CAAMA Productions); recorded over 40 Aboriginal artists on the first Aboriginal-owned recording label (CAAMA Music) and successfully bid for a licence to build and operate the only Aboriginal-owned satellite television service in the country (Imparja Television). Working with Freda during those extraordinarily productive years was without doubt

CAAMA staff at Gap Road Studios, 1984. From left: 'Bo' Barney, Issac Yamma, Erica Glynn, Philip Batty, Dean Sultan, Rodney Gooch, Freda Glynn, Janet Horhe (in front of Freda), Ronnie White, David Batty (obscured), Miss Peperril, Ivan Dixon, Christine Palmer, Clive Scollay and Rachel Wellington. (Photo: Russell Guy, courtesy Batty Collection)

Freda Glynn at Gap Road Studios, 1984. (Photo: Russell Guy, courtesy Batty Collection)

the most thrilling period of my life and, indeed, a great privilege.

CAAMA also trained a whole generation of young Indigenous people who went on to form the nucleus of today's Indigenous media culture in Australia. The long list includes: Freda's son, Warwick Thornton and his fellow Central Australian, Rachel Perkins, now both internationally acclaimed filmmakers; Freda's daughter Erica Glynn, former manager of Screen Australia's Indigenous Department and executive producer on ABC TV's *Redfern Now* (2015); screenwriter Stephen McGregor who, with another CAAMA trainee, David Tranter, co-wrote Thornton's *Sweet Country*. Other CAAMA trainees and former employees have also achieved outstanding success including Allen Collins (AACTA award for cinematography), Beck Cole (AACTA award for direction), Priscilla Collins (producer, Channel 9), Robyn Nardoo (director), Jason Ramp (cinematographer), David Liddle (journalist), and many more. More recently, a new generation of Indigenous media workers fostered by CAAMA are making their mark, including Freda's grandson Dylan River (director) and granddaughter, Tanith Glynn-Maloney (producer).

The evolution of CAAMA and the career of Freda Glynn as a progenitor of today's Indigenous media culture are

CAAMA trainees at CAAMA Studios, Little Sisters, 1987.
From left: Rachel Wellington, Erica Glynn.
(Photo: Philip Batty, courtesy Batty Collection)

Freda Glynn at CAAMA Studios, 1984.
(Photo: courtesy Batty Collection)

more or less synonymous. Although Freda makes the modest claim that her work at CAAMA represented just ten years in her long life they were, beyond doubt, ground-breaking years that helped change the way Australia sees itself. In this overview, I provide a personal reflection on both the evolution of CAAMA and my work with Freda.

* * *

I first met Freda in 1979 at a demonstration in Alice Springs. At the time, Central Australia was a politically fractured place. The Whitlam Labor Government's *Land Rights Bill* had inflamed pastoralists throughout the Northern Territory; the new Aboriginal Legal Aid service threatened the old local judicial system; bigoted police had come under investigation and missions had been abolished and their property handed over to Aboriginal organisations.

In this fraught atmosphere it was not unusual to find oneself at demonstrations. The one at which Freda and I met, was organised to protest against a group calling itself 'Citizens for Civilised Living'. The all-white 'Citizens' wanted to stop a government plan to move a small number of Aboriginal families from the squalid fringe camps of Alice Springs to the town's better-serviced white suburbs. A number of people – many of them so-called 'southern white stirrers' like myself – turned up to disrupt a meeting

From left: John Macumba, Freda Glynn, Philip Batty, at the opening of Imparja Television, 1988.
(Photo: Carmel Spears, courtesy Batty Collection)

of the 'citizens' . Freda was the only Aboriginal person at the protest and her bravery in confronting a hostile crowd of white people left a strong impression on me.

Eight months passed before I met Freda again; this time, at an event that would change both of us irrevocably. It was a tentative public meeting held in Alice Springs to discuss the formation of an organisation that proposed to work towards the establishment of an Aboriginal voice in the media.

The meeting was organised by me and a gregarious Aboriginal man from Oodnadatta, John Macumba. Our first few attempts to hold the meeting failed but on the third try, a number of Aboriginal people attended, including Freda, who voted with the majority to form a new organisation, tentatively named the Central Australian Aboriginal Media Association.

At the time, Freda was a single mother with five children: Sue, Erica, Scott, Robert and Warwick (then a ten-year-old boy). She had separated from her husband, Bob Thornton, and was cleaning hotels to support her family as sole breadwinner. This made any full time involvement in CAAMA impossible. Although she attended CAAMA committee meetings and helped where she could, it would be another 18 months before Freda took up the position of co-director of the new organisation.

In the interim, John Macumba played an invaluable role as we established the basic foundations of CAAMA. Certainly, without his seminal contribution, the organisation may not have survived its shaky beginnings. At one of the public meetings we organised to drum up support for CAAMA. John encapsulated the new organisations objectives when he said, 'We the Aboriginal people ... have been bombarded with just white European media ... and it is very important that we set up our own media association ... so that we can hear and see ourselves ... and keep our traditions alive.'

A brief summary of John's energetic commitment to

the organisation's early development is essential if we are to understand the evolution of CAAMA. Indeed, if the ten years I later spent working with Freda was the most thrilling decade of my life, the 18 months I spent working with John were the most intense.

When I met John in early 1980, he had only recently moved to Alice Springs with his wife Ellen and their three children. As a boy, he had been fostered out to an Adelaide family and spent most of his childhood in the city. He now wished to reconnect with the Aboriginal community in Central Australia and, as he said, 'shake things up'. By contrast, I was an over-radicalised young whitefella from Sydney who had grown up during the Vietnam War era. Three years before meeting John I had taken up a teaching job at the Aboriginal community of Papunya, 300 kilometres west of Alice Springs. I was shocked at what I perceived to be the oppressive conditions under which Aboriginal people lived at Papunya and many other communities in the region. This kindled a latent activism within me that I took to Alice Springs after leaving Papunya.

In early 1980, John and I happened to meet at a house party in Alice Springs and soon found that we shared an interest in media and its potential power to alter the status quo. Not long after our encounter, we began working together on *The Aboriginal Half Hour*, a weekly program broadcast through the commercial radio station, 8HA. The program was an initiative of the Northern Territory Education Department, due mainly to the efforts of Chris Majewski, a senior officer in the department. The show had a large and responsive following, which was not surprising given the fact that over half the population of Central Australia was then Aboriginal.

From the outset of our collaboration, John and I had ambitions that went far beyond the *Half Hour*. We spent many nights around a campfire while living at Basso's Farm, an abandoned artist's colony on the outskirts of Alice Springs. We were trying to work out how to establish, in the absence of any precedents, an Aboriginal-owned broadcasting station and video production facility. Our relatively recent move to Alice Springs and resulting lack of long-term connection with the local Aboriginal community was also problematic. Some members of this community viewed with suspicion anyone who claimed to act on their behalf, whether black or white. Nonetheless, the community meeting we organised to discuss our proposal and, more particularly, Freda's membership of the new body, resolved this issue.

Freda had deep connections with the people and

history of Central Australia, which gave the fledgling media organisation a secure grounding in the Alice Springs Aboriginal community; something that was of fundamental importance if the organisation was to get off the ground. Certainly, she had a remarkably eventful life growing up in the Central Australian region.

* * *

Freda was born on Woodgreen station, north of Alice Springs, in 1939. Her mother, Topsy Glynn, was a traditional Kaytetye woman who spoke several Aboriginal languages before English. Topsy received training at the station as a cook and subsequently worked for the owners. Freda's father, Alfred Price, was the son of Frederick Price, the second last postmaster of the Overland Telegraph Station in Alice Springs. Freda, or more correctly, Alfreda, was given the female version of her father's name, Alfred. Freda's only sibling, her older sister, Rona, was fathered by Alfred's brother, Ronald.

As an infant, Freda was afflicted with a life-threatening illness and was sent, tucked up in a wooden egg box, to the 'Bungalow' (aka 'The Half-caste Institution') in Alice Springs to receive urgent medical care, accompanied by Rona and her mother. As Freda required prolonged care, her mother was allowed to stay at the Bungalow where she was later employed as housekeeper and head cook. Freda says that this was 'the best thing that could have happened to me and my family' as it opened up the possibility of education, employment and a better life in Alice Springs. Her mother had no wish to return to Woodgreen station despite the owner's repeated requests to the welfare authorities to have her returned. Like other Aboriginal people, the Bungalow offered Freda and her family what Freda describes as a 'safe and secure home' away from what was then a harsh physical and social environment.

When war broke out in 1942, a Japanese invasion of the Northern Territory was a real possibility and most of the civilian population of Alice Springs were evacuated to the southern capitals. Freda's family was sent to Moree in New South Wales, and later billeted with the Lindemans, a family of wealthy wine merchants, in Vaucluse, Sydney. Freda's mother's reputation as an accomplished cook seems to have preceded her as she was employed as head chef and housekeeper at the Lindeman establishment. The Lindemans had a close connection with the Sydney art world and several portraits were produced of Freda as a young girl during their stay; one of which later found its way into the collection of the Art Gallery of NSW.

Returning to Alice Springs in 1949, Freda and her sister

were enrolled at St Mary's Children's Home, run by the Church of England Missionary Society. It was a place for which Freda still holds fond memories, particularly for its head, Sister Eileen Heath, with whom Freda kept in touch throughout her life. Freda's mother worked at St Mary's for several years, again as a cook, and was thus able to see and talk with her daughters on a daily basis. Freda says that her mother was 'with us all the time' when they were growing up and that she never 'took much notice of the welfare people' with whom she was 'always arguing'.

After leaving St Mary's in the mid-1950s, Freda was immediately offered training and a job at the only photographic studio in Alice Springs, and for 17 years she captured practically every baptism, wedding and birthday in the town. Working alone in the studio's darkroom, Freda enjoyed listening to the ABC, then the only radio service available in Alice Springs. She says that this gave her a 'great education' about the world beyond the confines of Central Australia.

Remarkably, in 1960, Freda's mother secured a bank loan to purchase a house in Alice Springs – the first Aboriginal woman in the Territory to do so – and paid off the loan in three years. Freda's sister, Rona, was an equally remarkable person. She was an outstanding school pupil who became the first Indigenous teacher in the Northern Territory. She also wrote a newspaper column for the local *Centralian Advocate*. Rona later studied nursing in Melbourne and New Zealand and was such an exemplary student that she was later appointed head of the maternity ward at Alice Springs Hospital. Although she supervised over 2000 births, Rona died in tragic circumstances, giving birth to her own child in 1965. The Rona Glynn Pre-school in Alice Springs was named in her honour.

With the election of the federal Labor Government in 1972 and the creation of the first federal Department of Aboriginal Affairs (DAA), people like Freda were in demand. Employed by the Department in the mid-1970s, she received training in development management at the South Australian Institute of Technology in the Task Force program. She was subsequently offered work back in Alice Springs as a Community Development Officer, assisting people living on the town's fringe camps.

It was during this period that I first met Freda at the demonstration against the 'Citizens for Civilised Living', and a few months later, at the community meeting to establish CAAMA. As already indicated, she was working full time to support her five children and was only able to participate in monthly CAAMA meetings and assist John and myself, on occasion, with the *Aboriginal Half Hour*. For the time being, John and I would continue to work on the foundation of CAAMA.

* * *

In mid-February 1980, we presented a written submission to the Department of Aboriginal Affairs announcing the formation of CAAMA and seeking financial support. The Minister for Aboriginal Affairs in the Liberal Fraser Government, Fred Chaney, was receptive but felt that his colleague, Minster for Communications Tony Staley, should fund CAAMA.

While the ministers debated their respective responsibilities, the Institute for Aboriginal Development (IAD) in Alice Springs offered their support. They hired filmmaker Clive Scollay to organise a CAAMA media tour of public broadcasting stations in Canberra, Sydney and Melbourne and, more significantly, to arrange meetings with Chaney and Staley (then a Cabinet minister) to push CAAMA's case.

Obligingly, the ministers agreed to meet the CAAMA delegation at Parliament House in early April. While Chaney was somewhat equivocal, offering little support for CAAMA, the opposite was true of Staley. When we entered his office, he said, with his feet on his ministerial desk,

'The government would like to offer you a gift: the old ABC studios and broadcasting facilities in Alice Springs,' and with that, he lit up a cigar. Stunned at such generosity, we thanked Staley and headed back to Alice Springs. In the meantime, he issued a press release notifying the public of his magnanimous offer. However, on inspecting the 'studios' we discovered that they were in a ruinous state and devoid of any equipment. Contact was immediately made with Staley's office to alert him to the real state of the 'gift'.

Six weeks later, on 28 May, Staley and Chaney flew to Alice Springs to speak with us. During this critically important meeting, it was resolved that the old studios would be renovated and production equipment installed for CAAMA's use; that the new ABC studios and offices in Alice Springs would be made available to CAAMA while the renovations to the old studios were completed; and that DAA would consider funding CAAMA's production and operational costs. I still find it surprising, if not astonishing, that a small, untested group from the desert was able to extract support from some of the most powerful political figures in the nation, including a Cabinet minister. Such, perhaps, was the goodwill that then existed towards Aboriginal people.

At about the same time, the federal government

established a committee of inquiry into the ABC (the Dix Committee) and it happened to be holding a hearing in Alice Springs. This represented an unprecedented opportunity for CAAMA, then the only Aboriginal media organisation in the country. John delivered a powerful speech at the hearing, pointing out that the ABC was providing no Aboriginal programming in the country and that it must immediately rectify this 'appalling oversight'. Two ABC executives present at the hearing – John Newsome and John Hartley – later recalled that John's speech hit them 'like a ton of bricks'.

Within a matter of months, CAAMA was contracted to produce radio programming on the local ABC outlet (8AL) and the ABC itself planned to launch its own pilot Aboriginal radio program through the same station and on a national basis. This had major repercussions for Freda. The ABC offered her training and a full-time position at the ABC producing and presenting their local program, which she accepted.

Much else was undertaken during this brief, hectic period: CAAMA played a role in establishing Alice Spring's first public radio station, 8CCC; the first Indigenous media training programs were created; licence applications were submitted; radio programs were produced; building and equipment were installed; and much more. Indeed, from January 1980 to June 1981, CAAMA went from nothing but an idea through to a burgeoning organisation, producing and broadcasting daily radio programming in four Aboriginal languages through three outlets: the public station, 8CCC, the regional ABC station, 8AL and the commercial station, 8HA.

In May 1981, John decided to leave CAAMA and Alice Springs. He had been offered a substantial managerial position that he could not refuse in his home town, Oodnadatta. Despite my pleadings, he headed south with his family and remained there for several years with occasional visits to Alice Springs. Sadly, John passed away in 2010 at a relatively young age. He will always be remembered for his pioneering efforts at CAAMA and in promoting Aboriginal participation in the media in general.

* * *

Although Freda was now employed full time at the ABC, she continued to attend CAAMA meetings. However, with the unexpected departure of John, the question of her taking a more hands-on role with CAAMA arose. Indeed, I was concerned that if someone could not be found to replace John, CAAMA might falter. Fortunately, Freda readily agreed to leave the ABC and take up the position of co-director of CAAMA in July 1981.

A good start had been made in laying the foundations of CAAMA, but the work of turning it into an organisation with its own independent radio and television services, with a strong production capability and well-resourced training program was yet to be achieved and it was to this end that Freda and I worked together up until the end of the 1980s.

Similar in some ways to my time with John, working with Freda entailed the writing of numerous submissions and attendance at countless meetings with government officials, politicians, media groups, Aboriginal organisations and many other people and bodies. In all this work, one could say that I supplied the bullets and Freda fired them, at least that's how we both saw our working relationship, more or less.

One of our most important submissions at this time (presented to the federal government in 1983) focused on Australia's forthcoming national satellite, AUSSAT, due to be launched in 1985. We pointed out in the submission that the satellite would, for the first time, make available a wide range of telecommunication services, including TV, to hundreds of remote Aboriginal communities. We insisted that these communities should be afforded some measure of control over what we described as the 'avalanche' of television about to pour into their homes. We also argued that Aboriginal people should be given the ability to produce television programming on their own terms and in their own languages as a way of moderating this forthcoming 'cultural televisual dominance'.

To back up these arguments, Freda and I attended a number conferences and seminars in the southern capitals where Freda made impassioned speeches about the potential impact of the satellite. At this point, the federal government was still making up its mind about how AUSSAT would be regulated and who would have access to it.

Our arguments concerning the need for Aboriginal production of Aboriginal programming in the face of the impending satellite were also put to the Australian Film Commission (AFC). Responding positively, the AFC, then headed up by Cathy Robinson, and later Kim Williams, provided CAAMA with enough funding to establish the CAAMA Video Unit at the end of 1983 (later, CAAMA Productions Pty Ltd). Clive Scollay was re-engaged to set up the Unit with four Aboriginal trainees. While technically 'trainees', they were thrown into intensive production work, including a number of contracts for government departments. One of the trainees was Erica Glynn. It now seems to me that the fast and often bumpy learning curve she and the other trainees experienced in the Unit proved to be a valuable asset in future employment. Certainly, it gave Erica the skills she later applied with great dexterity as an executive producer and manager of the Indigenous Department at Screen Australia.

Moves were also made in 1983 to establish CAAMA's own independent radio broadcasting network. A detailed application was made late that year to the Australian Broadcasting Tribunal (ABT) for a licence to operate a public radio station in Alice Springs with repeaters at the Aboriginal communities of Hermannsburg, Ali Curung and Santa Teresa. A year later, the ABT convened a public hearing in Alice Springs at which Aboriginal organisations and people throughout the Northern Territory came to speak in support of the application, including Pat Dodson, then director of the Central Land Council. After a brief deliberation, the ABT officially awarded CAAMA its long-awaited broadcasting licence in September 1984; the first-ever awarded to an Aboriginal organisation. In making its decision, the chairman of the ABT, David Jones, said it was 'an historic occasion in Australian broadcasting'

By May 1985, CAAMA's radio network, 8KIN-FM, had been installed and tested and John Macumba was invited back from Oodnadatta to officially launch the station on the 27 May. To celebrate this momentous occasion, we invited numerous Aboriginal bands, choirs, solo artists and traditional dancers from communities throughout Central Australia to perform on stage in front of the new station. Such was the enthusiasm of the enormous crowd that attended the opening that it proved almost impossible to bring the celebrations to a close. I remember Freda, standing on the stage as night fell, trying to persuade thousands of people to go home – with little success.

The new station was located in Little Sisters, a renovated former Catholic convent on the southern outskirts of Alice Springs, next to a town camp, also named Little Sisters, which could sometimes become extremely rowdy. On occasion, when one of the radio announcers failed to turn up, Freda would grab her teenage son Warwick to fill in. This experience later formed the basis of Warwick's award-winning short, *Green Bush* (2005).

The old convent also accommodated the CAAMA video unit, audio-visual library, administrative offices and other facilities. In 1984, a recording studio was constructed next to the convent and a recording label, CAAMA Music, created. Within three years the label had grown into a substantial business, selling more than 30,000 cassettes and CDs annually, from a catalogue of some 40 albums.

The recording studio was managed by music producer Bill Davis, working with Aboriginal trainees including Mark Manolis who later found work in the recording industry. Bill and his team later produced a series of award-winning radio programs for schools located in Aboriginal communities throughout the Northern Territory known as *Bushfire Radio.*

The launch of the 8KIN network and CAAMA Music label were far from the only undertakings initiated by CAAMA at this time. Our original bid to obtain access to the national satellite, AUSSAT, as outlined in CAAMA's 1982 submission, took a new turn. In 1984, the federal government finally made a decision about who would have access to AUSSAT.

Briefly, Minister for Communications Michael Duffy decided that licences would only be granted to commercial television operators to provide services from the satellite. Further, the Australian Broadcasting Tribunal would decide who was to be awarded these licences through a competitive process after public hearings. If anyone else wanted access to the satellite, they would have to negotiate with the successful licensees.

This meant that community-based bodies like CAAMA would have to beg these commercial operators for access with no guarantee of success. It seemed, at the time, as if we were completely locked out. There was however one small chink in this seemingly impenetrable armour. CAAMA could create its own commercial TV company and bid for one of the licences in its own right and thus obtain unfettered access. Indeed, one of the satellite's service areas covered all of those towns and regions that CAAMA had always wished to reach.

This created a huge dilemma. CAAMA had no interest in operating a commercial TV service, but if it did not submit a licence application it would have no guaranteed access to the satellite. I remember having long, anxious discussions with Freda and the CAAMA committee about whether to apply for the licence. We would have to broadcast predominantly commercial television programming, yet CAAMA was established to counter such material. In short, we would be forced to sup with the devil. In the end, we decided to apply for the licence as there was no alternative. Although we did not know it at the time, this decision would lead, through a complex, painful route, to my departure from CAAMA, as well as Freda's.

A communications consultant, Brian Walsh, was hired to co-ordinate the bid and a substantial two-volume application was eventually delivered by hand to the ABT's

Sydney office, less than an hour before applications closed in late December 1984. It contained proposals to broadcast a mix of community television programming, along with mandatory commercial material, catering to both the Aboriginal audience (then about 35% of the total), and non-Aboriginal viewers. We created, on paper, a television company, Imparja (meaning 'track' in the Arrernte language) to facilitate the bid. One small problem remained, however, CAAMA had no money to actually establish the service.

With the application securely lodged, we waited for the ABT to set a licence hearing date. In the meantime, Freda and I conducted a tour of Indigenous television satellite services in North America. Whilst in Canada, we visited the remote Arctic Circle where satellite technology had been delivering TV programming in the Inuit language for many years. Here, we were warmly welcomed by representatives of the Inuit Broadcasting Corporation who offered to appear at the hearing (via satellite) in support our application. The insights gained during the trip eradicated any lingering doubts about our decision to apply for the satellite TV licence; it also gave us plenty of ammunition to present at the forthcoming hearings.

The first hearing was held on 6 August 1985 in Alice

Springs. Two contenders had applied for the licence, CAAMA and the Darwin-based commercial TV station, Channel 8, which was acquired in the middle of the hearing by media magnet and Australia's richest man, Kerry Packer. We had 24 Aboriginal and non-Aboriginal witnesses to support our case, including eye surgeon, Fred Hollows; the former head of the reserve bank, H.C. 'Nugget' Coombs; Minister for Education in the South Australian government, Lynn Arnold, (later premier of that state); Rosemarie Kuptana, head of the Inuit Broadcasting Corporation (via satellite); and many Aboriginal community representatives.

While we were able to put forward a convincing case in terms of our Aboriginal programming and special audience needs, we did not of course have experience in operating a television station. More problematically, we had been unable to secure financial support, despite several funding submissions to the federal government. In sharp contrast, Channel 8 had the required funds and the technical experience. They planned to relay their existing commercial television material through the new satellite service, together with some local news, but there would be no programming for the substantial Aboriginal audience.

Freda and I held out little hope of winning the bid, in fact no one on our team did. We were therefore astonished when the ABT decided that neither CAAMA nor Channel 8 qualified for the licence and that another hearing would be called to decide the matter. In short, CAAMA had 'impressive' programming, but zero finance, while Channel 8 possessed the finance, but no Aboriginal programming. The next hearing was set down for 17 March 1986, giving both parties six months to re-boot their applications. As the communications academic Eric Michaels suggested, the ABT sent both applicants on a 'treasure hunt': 'CAAMA had to come back with six million dollars', while Channel 8 had 'to find some Aboriginal content'.

With the real prospect of winning the licence, Freda, myself and other CAAMA staff (including 'Shorty' O'Neil, formerly of the North Queensland Land Council), organised an intensive round of new meetings with government funding bodies. In the end, we were able to obtain an undertaking that if CAAMA won the licence, the funds would be forthcoming, subject to ministerial approval. About 30% of this money was to come from the Australian Bicentennial Authority, which had been established to celebrate, in 1988, the 200th anniversary of European settlement in Australia. The Authority had substantial funding for 'nationally focused' Aboriginal projects and an Aboriginal-owned satellite television service appeared to fit the bill.

Some city-based Aboriginal groups protested against CAAMA accepting the bicentennial 'blood money' and, on several occasions, Freda fronted up to these groups to argue that all government funding to Aboriginal organisations could be described as 'blood money'. Indeed, at a particularly hostile meeting, I remember thinking back to the first time I met Freda when she was confronted by the all-white Citizens for Civilised Living. On this occasion, it was an all-Aboriginal crowd she faced with the same bravery.

Following the second, tumultuous hearing, the ABT awarded the licence to CAAMA in August 1986, stating that 'on balance', CAAMA could provide a more 'comprehensive' service. Channel 8 had made some limited attempt to develop Aboriginal programming but it failed to impress the ABT. Miraculously, once we had secured the license, the funding bodies made good on their promise to provide the required $6 million funds. The decision produced a near hysterical response from the conservative Northern Territory Government. As recorded in Hansard, Chief Minister Ian Tuxworth thundered, 'This is a joke ... giving a television signal that covers one-third of the Australian continent to a group ... that is incapable, incompetent and unfinancial (*sic*), is madness.'

Channel 8 launched an appeal against the decision, but that too failed. By the end of 1986, CAAMA was ready to build its own satellite service, Imparja Television.

* * *

Along with the licence came $3.5 million in promised funding to train over 30 Aboriginal 'media cadets' in association with the Australian Film Television and Radio School, to be coordinated by the School's Julie Wiggins. Two of these trainees were Warwick Thornton and Rachel Perkins.

One could say that Warwick grew up with CAAMA. Indeed, Freda used to refer to him and his sister Erica as her 'CAAMA babies'. As a 12-year-old, Warwick could often be found riding his BMX bike around the CAAMA radio studios, pestering his mother. As we have seen, his initial role at CAAMA was that of a 'fill-in' radio announcer, up until he had his own program. When he took up one of the new traineeships after the license victory, he received on-the-job training, using the CAAMA video unit's new camera equipment. It was clear from the outset that he had a particularly acute 'eye' and aesthetic sensibility, which would lead him onto a successful career. Rachel Perkins had grown up in the southern cities, but she too had close ties with Central Australia. Her famous activist father, Charlie

Perkins, was born in the region and, like Freda, had spent time as a child at the Bungalow home in Alice Springs. Rachel had quite different interests to Warwick. When I first met her, she was halfway through a Dostoevsky novel and already talking about films she planned to make. My immediate thought was, this young woman will go far.

With the training program underway, work began on the establishment of Imparja TV, and after a frantic 12 months or so, Imparja went to air on 15 January 1988. Rachel's father, then head of the Aboriginal Development Commission, officially launched the station before a crowd of some 500 guests. In a subsequent press interview, Freda said: 'After all the hard work, this is a proud moment for our mob.'

And, indeed, it was.

During the first 18 months of Imparja's on-air operations, we lived up to our promise to broadcast a mix of Aboriginal programming and commercial fare. Using Imparja TV's production studios, the CAAMA Video Unit produced two weekly programs: *Urrpeye (Messenger)*, a current affairs show, and *Nganampa Anwernekenhe (Ours)*, presented in three Aboriginal languages (*Arrernte*, *Pitjantjatjara* and *Warlpiri*), focusing on news and events in local Aboriginal communities. The Unit also produced a number of short segments on Aboriginal health, welfare services, legal aid, nutrition and child care that were broadcast throughout all Imparja programming. Further, the 8KIN network could now be heard right across the Northern Territory and South Australia via Imparja's satellite signal.

Unfortunately, by the end of 1990, a serious internal argument had arisen within CAAMA concerning the operations of Imparja TV. Briefly, as the service developed, it came under pressure to maximise its commercial income. This had an increasingly detrimental effect on the production of Aboriginal programming. For example, more priority was given to the production of local advertisements on equipment originally purchased through funds intended for the creation of Aboriginal programming. Freda and I insisted that Imparja should remain true to its original intentions of providing quality Aboriginal programming, along with the commercial fare. This, we argued, was the reason we had won the license. Our opponents claimed, however, that as Imparja was licensed as a commercial television station, commercial considerations should take priority.

When the dispute was finally presented to members of the CAAMA committee, they failed to support us, leading to our eventual resignations. Only later did we discover that senior government figures had surreptitiously communicated with committee members recommending our removal. They were apparently concerned that our actions could lead to the collapse of Imparja and a major embarrassment for the government.

While this is not the place to analyse the events surrounding our departure, one thing is clear, after we left, locally made Aboriginal programming on Imparja eventually disappeared and what had been hailed as a 'flagship of Aboriginal culture', became a very basic commercial TV station. This was a great tragedy, given the enormous potential Imparja had for delivering targeted programming to Indigenous communities. Nonetheless, there were several positive outcomes from this debacle: some of the annual profits from Imparja funded other CAAMA projects; the $3.5 million for CAAMA's training program would not have been made available if we had failed to win Imparja's license, and the basic fact that CAAMA owned a satellite service set a precedent for similar services in the future.

Setting aside Imparja, less than eight years after the first tentative moves to establish CAAMA, the organisation was operating a radio network (8KIN-FM) that could be heard over a third of the Australian continent; a video and television production company (CAAMA Productions); a music recording and distribution business (CAAMA Music); and three retail outlets (CAAMA Shops). Furthermore, the immense video, audio and musical archive produced by CAAMA over this decade now constitutes a national treasure house of Indigenous culture, history and heritage that has continued to expand.

We were also engaged in a major training program that would eventually produce a generation of young Indigenous people who would go on to form the bedrock of today's Indigenous media culture in Australia. Indeed, former trainees and employees of CAAMA can be found throughout Australia's broadcasting and film world. Moreover, following CAAMA's example, over a hundred other independent Aboriginal media and broadcasting services have emerged across Australia, which set the stage for the launch of the Indigenous Community Television network (ICTV) and the National Indigenous Television network (NITV), both of which now provide programming for remote Aboriginal communities and a national audience.

Working with Freda and many other people on these developments had been a wild and incredibly productive journey that achieved outcomes we could never have imagined possible. For Freda – born on a remote station and transferred in an egg carton to Alice Springs as a baby – these achievements are even more outstanding. I will always cherish these years spent with Freda and our enduring friendship.

Distinguished Professor **Larissa Behrendt** is a Gamilaroi/Eualeyai woman and an academic, filmmaker and writer. She is writer and director of the documentary *After the Apology* (2017).

standing on the shoulders of giants

Larissa Behrendt

Many Aboriginal nations are matrilineal; matriarchs are a central and powerful force in our cultures. Perhaps it explains why our cultures have sustained over 65,000 years.

Freda Glynn epitomises strong leadership, particularly in her visionary way of considering not just her own generation and that of her children but ensuring that she leaves a legacy for many generations to come.

Her role in establishing CAAMA ensured there was an institution that could foster Indigenous storytelling in a way that ensured community control over those stories – and ensured the development of generations of storytellers. CAAMA is self-determination in action. It helps facilitate vibrant cultures and their transmission and has been especially strong in recording Indigenous languages. When one considers the way in which Aboriginal people have had their images and stories appropriated, the importance of Indigenous agency in film, radio, television and other forms of digital storytelling is fundamentally an act of resistance, a reassertion of sovereignty.

I was in a unique position to understand the deeper importance of Freda Glynn's vision when I, as inaugural chair of NITV, could see how it led the Indigenous media world in terms of infrastructure and content generation. And I find myself with a renewed appreciation of her legacy as filmmaking has taken a more central role in my own creative practice in recent years. CAAMA has provided for me, like it has for so many other emerging Aboriginal and Torres Strait Islander filmmakers, opportunities to work and gain experience in a highly competitive industry – and in a way that allows us to work with stories that have deep meaning for us.

There is an important parallel in Freda Glynn's life work with that of other trailblazers of her generation. I think of her on the same echelon as the Aboriginal men and women who set up the Aboriginal medical services, the Aboriginal legal services, and the many other community-controlled organisations. It was a generation that understood the importance of Aboriginal and Torres Strait Islander people being centrally involved in the institutions that affect us the most and the need to ensure that our voices are heard and are persuasive.

And perhaps one of the reasons that Freda Glynn sits so easily in this company is because she was of the generation that was so active in building organisations and institutions and by doing that completely changed the playing field for future generations. Doors were opened for their children that had been previously closed to them. In this way she reminds me very much of my father who, denied further education and without tertiary qualifications of his own, established the Aboriginal Research and Resource Centre at the University of New South Wales. It made my step into university studies – and into a career in academia – easier, perhaps even inevitable! We as the children of such people stand on the shoulders of giants.

And so we see Freda's own children stand on those shoulders, in a way where *their* work continues to push the boundaries and break further barriers but always keeps a true compass with the cultural values of their heritage. This is evident even in recent work. Erica Glynn must be one of the hardest working directors in Australia.

In her 2017 documentary, *In My Own Words*, she creates a polemic about the importance of literacy as a means of self-expression and self-determination, an explanation of the way in which access to education opens opportunity but can also increase the ability to remain strong in your own culture.

Similarly, Warwick Thornton's *We Don't Need A Map* (2017) confronts appropriation of the Southern Cross as a racist icon and reclaims the ground for the cultural stories that have guided our ancestors for tens of millennia and at the same time, repositioned Indigenous voice.

Both recent works pay homage in different ways to the concepts of challenging entrenched societal barriers and reframing the conversation from a position that centralises the Indigenous worldview. And that in no way detracts from the inherent and innate talent that Erica and Warwick have as auteurs in their own right.

In some ways it seems strange to talk of two generations of an Aboriginal family – three if you include Dylan River and Tanith Glynn-Maloney, who are leading talents of their generation. 'Dynasty' is not a term we have in our Aboriginal culture. We have totems, clans, skin names and moieties – concepts that are more relational than hierarchical. And in this way, we can more profoundly celebrate the transmission of story from one generation to another and know that we remain custodians of story. It's in our DNA.

None of this stops us from paying a deep respect to those who show a real and natural talent for it. But it also beholds us to take a moment to pay respect to those who take significant steps to ensure those cycles continue. Freda Glynn AM deserves many of those moments.

Kim Williams, AM,

has had a long involvement in the arts and media and held various leadership positions since the late 1970s, including as CEO at News Corp Australia, FOXTEL, Fox Studios Australia, the Australian Film Commission, Southern Star Entertainment and Musica Viva. He has served on many boards and is now chairman of Thomson Reuters Trustees and an AFL Commissioner. MUP published his book *Rules of Engagement* in 2014.

Freda Glynn, CAAMA and the creation of Imparja

Kim Williams, AM

I met Freda Glynn in my first year at the then Australian Film Commission (AFC). The Commission was the Commonwealth's statutory authority for support (through funding and policy) of the Australian film and television production industry and had a broad, strong set of powers which, in summary, provided support for the production, distribution, promotion and broadcasting of Australian programs. Freda was to ensure we tested our legislative powers to their limit. She was determined and she was going to make a real impact on Indigenous broadcasting – of that there was no doubt. Now, please note, all I write here needs one simple qualification – it is written through a 34-year filter of personal memory (and we all know that while the big picture is usually clear, the detail can become somewhat less so!). So with that simple stipulation, on to my memory of Freda, CAAMA and Imparja.

I had been appointed as the CEO of the AFC in late 1983 and assumed the role in early 1984 as a 31-year-old. I was inexperienced and quickly needed to master a large number of policy matters, parliamentary procedures and protocols, public sector protocols and a broad range of AFC support programs. Not to mention the diversity of individuals in Australian film and television life at that time. But Freda made sure that Indigenous issues were near the top of the priority list from the start.

I had assistance from many people at the AFC, the Home Affairs Department and its then minister, Barry Cohen, and some fine politicians who were supportive towards a young greenhorn and offered constructive, often quite meaty assistance in getting some formidable policy matters and programs supported. There was also never-ending 'assistance' (you get a surfeit of 'help' in a job like that) from filmmakers, bureaucrats, politicians and public commentators with extensive frank feedback across the length and breadth of Australia. I was often suffocated with the 'kindness of supplicants' eager to receive support from the AFC's various programs. Freda wasn't like that mob – her advocacy was always calm, considered and rooted in the justness of her case.

The Film Commission had two primary funding arms – the Film Development Branch (which included a Special Production Fund), to develop and invest in a range of mainstream adult and children's film, and television production, including documentary.

Then there was the independent Creative Development Branch, which was geared to fund cultural organisations in the sector (such as the Australian Film Institute and a wide variety of state-based organisations) and to backing more experimental production work.

A marketing division (which supported Australian-produced film and television work internationally) and the national film production house – Film Australia – completed the AFC. All these arms of the Commission had different personalities working in their programs, the programs themselves differed, and their impact. Freda made it her job to know the key players.

The work of the Creative Development Branch was always among the most diverse, stimulating and, from a public perspective, confronting and controversial. Freda was an ardent and effective advocate who indefatigably lobbied for more money to be spent on Aboriginal and Torres

Strait Islander endeavour generally, and very specifically for activity in Central Australia. She found a ready and committed partner in the director of that branch, Vicki Molloy.

Vicki was magnificently feisty and deeply committed to a range of social initiatives which would secure a better position for women and Indigenous filmmakers in the AFC's priorities – frankly it wasn't a hard case to sell as the commissioners were as one in wanting to see real impact investment in both areas.

Philip Batty with John Macumba and later joined by Freda, had already founded the Central Australian Aboriginal Media Association Group of Companies (CAAMA) in 1980. Radio services in different languages soon followed. Freda had wanted to ensure that CAAMA's remarkable vitality and grand ambition for influence, specifically through broadcasting and video, was enhanced with better funding and the allocation of a Remote Area Commercial Television Licence (RCTS).

In October 1984, Minister for Communication Michael Duffy directed the Australian Broadcasting Tribunal (ABT) to hold an inquiry to determine who would be the most appropriate RCTS licensees. The Tribunal had to report by 1 April 1985 and have regard of a detailed policy statement set out to parliament. It was far-reaching stuff. The government also expected the first of these new services to be operational by 1 January 1986. So, it all needed to happen very quickly.

Freda sought the support of a number of organisations including the AFC in a wildly ambitious objective: one of the licences – that for Central Australia – should be under Aboriginal control. It seems an easy decision now, but I can assure you it was one many found confronting 34 years ago. There were issues of addressing the immense technical complexities and the need for programming skills of a high order and a vast body of material to broadcast.

Ministers such as Barry Cohen and Clyde Holding were professionally sceptical. While both had long histories of passionate commitment to meaningful substantial policy action for Aboriginal and Torres Strait Islanders, they had practical concerns about the danger inherent in any potential failure should the licence be awarded, and the service subsequently fail. Freda was undeterred. She marshalled forces to support the process of the inquiry, including spirited advocacy from Charlie Perkins (who was on the phone to me at least three or four times a week) and many others who have with the passage of time become supporting players in my feeble memory. In any case the AFC got right behind the process, made direct representation to the ABT and reassured ministers that it would all be a splendid success! The rest is history. Freda and her team won the licence, Imparja was born and programming in Indigenous languages on the service was there from the outset.

It is a remarkable story and testament to persistent advocacy of the most persuasive kind. Freda Glynn is truly one of a kind and I would think one would be wise to heed her counsel, always. She is a visionary – a role model of rare and exemplary dimension where the resonances of her passion and impact live long and strong – including through her outstandingly creative children Warwick Thornton and Erica Glynn, whose work stands proudly beside that of their mother.

Steven McGregor

is an award-winning writer and director across television and feature film, both documentary and fiction. He co-wrote *Sweet Country* (dir. Warwick Thornton). His credits include *Warriors, Blue Water Empire, Mystery Road, Redfern Now, Servant or Slave* and *My Brother Vinnie.*

don't fuck it up

Steven McGregor

In the 1990s I moved from Darwin to Alice Springs to work at Imparja television as news camera/editor. I'd heard a lot about CAAMA over the years and seen their television crews working in Darwin. I wanted to be a part of that and when the job came up at Imparja, I jumped at it.

It was then I first met Warwick, Freda and Erica. Freda was a force but she was also a little scary and spoke her mind. Warwick once asked me, 'Have you ever been sacked by your mother?' I said no and he replied, 'I've been sacked three times from CAAMA by my mother.' OK.

Over the years I've become very close to the family and have worked on many productions with them. The most recent is *Sweet Country*, which I co-wrote with David

Tranter and Warwick directed. After Warwick read the script he sent me a text and said, 'I love it and I want to direct it.' I replied, 'Don't fuck it up.' He didn't. *Sweet Country* has done well. I remember the world premiere at Venice in 2017. We were all dressed up in suits, styling it up on the red carpet, cameras going off everywhere. We all sort of looked at each and thought, Waaa shame job, what are we doing here? but deadly.

It's always a pleasure seeing Freda, which usually happens at Erica's place in Sydney where Warwick is cooking up a storm making a big mess and telling people to piss off if they lift the lid off a pot to check what's on offer.

Freda's face lights up when we all sit around talking shit and she always asks me what I've been working on. When I tell her she smiles and says, 'I'm so proud of all my CAAMA family, it's what I wanted CAAMA to be, to give people a voice to tell their stories.'

Thanks, Nanna Freda.

David Tranter

is a documentary filmmaker and Australia's leading Aboriginal sound recordist. He won an AFI Award, an Australian Screen Sound Award and was nominated for an IF Award For his work on Warwick Thornton's *Samson & Delilah*. In 2011, he was awarded the inaugural Bob Plasto Screen Award. *Sweet Country*, based on a story told to Tranter by his grandfather, is his feature screenwriting debut.

in at the deep end

David Tranter

I've been friends/family with the Glynn/Thornton family since I was a little kid in Alice Springs. We spent our time hanging around the streets and hills riding pushbikes and motorbikes, and swimming at Wiggly's waterhole – when not at school, of course.

There were always kids around the dinner table at Freda's and we all got a feed. It was competitive, each kid keeping an eye on each other's plate to see if that last chop was going to get eaten or that glass of cordial was going to get drunk.

When I first worked at CAAMA I was the bus driver picking up the language speakers to take them into CAAMA. I used to see the video crews going out bush and when I was asked if I wanted to train as a sound recordist I said yes. I just wanted to go bush really.

I spent many months on the road with Warwick and Erica out bush filming language programs. It is where we all cut our teeth, learnt our craft. Freda threw us all in the deep end, it was sink or swim, no mollycoddling. At the time I didn't really take too much notice at what was being created, but looking back now I can see Freda had a vision, one that has given us all a platform to tell our stories, to share our stories.

One story that was told to me by my grandfather became the film *Sweet Country*, a script I co-wrote with Steven McGregor. After many years of development I got to stand on the red carpet at the world premiere of *Sweet Country* at the Venice Film Festival. Beside me were my brother boys, Warwick, his son Dylan, and McGregor. It was a moment I'll never forget, a moment I would never had experienced had Freda not thrown me in at the deep end to become a sound recordist. Thanks, Nanna Freda.

Lee-Ann Tjunypa Buckskin

is a Narungga, Wirangu, Wotjobaluk woman. She is currently executive consultant for the Aboriginal Screen Strategy with the South Australian Film Corporation, creative producer of Country Arts South Australia's three-year *Diggers Project* and co-chair of Tarnanthi, the Festival of Contemporary Aboriginal and Torres Strait Islander Visual Art in South Australia. She is also Deputy Chair of the Australia Council Board.

we must do more

Lee-Ann Tjunypa Buckskin

For women around the world, 2018 is a significant year. It is the 100-year anniversary of the suffragette movement. As well, it is the 2018 NAIDOC theme 'Because of her, we can'. With these important markers in mind, I find it incredibly frustrating that there is very little information regarding the extraordinary life and career of Freda Glynn AM. How can we truly know and celebrate our women if we don't reflect and celebrate their contributions to our everyday lives? It is another stark reminder to us all on how far we have to go to secure true equality for all. We cannot allow these stories to remain silent. We must do more, we must expect much more! We must not keep women's achievements silent in our country's history. Let's get writing, ladies!

Bridget Ikin

is an independent film producer, based in Sydney, whose award-winning credits include *Sherpa* (dir. Jen Peedom), *Look Both Ways* (dir. Sarah Watt), and *An Angel at my Table* (dir. Jane Campion). She also produces multi-screen moving image projects with artists, including Hossein Valamanesh, and Angelica Mesiti. She ran SBS Independent from 1996–2000, and was instrumental in commissioning many films from Indigenous filmmakers. In 2018, she was awarded an Honorary Doctorate from AFTRS.

the pathfinder: to see it is to be it

Bridget Ikin

In 1996 I was employed to run SBS Independent – the newly established commissioning arm of SBS Television. Until then, SBS TV was predominantly a broadcaster of programming from countries other than Australia, and in other languages. But with a very welcome injection of federal funding, SBS Independent enabled SBS TV to engage with and reflect more fully the many faces of Australia. Our small commissioning team was fired up to encourage filmmakers to tell their stories, from every corner of the country.

At that time, the groundbreaking *Sand to Celluloid* series had recently been completed, and it was a no-brainer for SBS Independent to forge a strong alliance with the

Australian Film Commission's Indigenous Branch for future collaborations – both drama and (later) documentary series. Their strategy of careful mentoring and hands-on training was bearing fruit already. SBS was the willing broadcaster: the filmmakers' voices were urgent, the films were fresh, lively and emotionally charged. These were such significant stories, and we were very keen to share them widely with audiences.

Shifting Sands came next; I was the commissioning editor. Erica Glynn's marvellous *My Bed, Your Bed* brought me to Alice Springs for the first (and most indelible) time in 1997, during its filming. Warwick Thornton shooting; Rachel Perkins the first assistant director. There was a palpable feeling of true teamwork ... and of promise. The multi-award-winning film is now a classic, and remains a favourite of mine. I saw first-hand the role that CAAMA was committed to (and had been since 1980), and I was in awe of the organisation's impact. But I wasn't yet aware of the influential role that Freda Glynn had been playing ...

Gradually, I pieced it together, becoming aware of Freda's powerful guiding hand. Freda, the visionary co-founder of CAAMA and mother to Warwick and Erica, gave early employment opportunities there to a host of filmmakers, including Warwick, Erica, Alan Collins, David Tranter,

Steven McGregor and Rachel Perkins. In the Australian Film Commission's 2007 publication *Dreaming in Motion*, Rachel articulated how significant Freda has been in her career: '[Freda] argued that in a world only recently, but now completely, dominated by another culture, it is critical for Indigenous Australians to have a voice. We, her Indigenous trainees at the time, were a conduit for that voice.'

I started to appreciate the scope and depth of Freda's vision: that storytelling (both on film and via radio) can make culture strong, while also bringing employment, empowerment and skills to talented young Indigenous people. Reflecting now on the mighty harvest of films that Freda's vision has spawned, it's abundantly clear that film can serve to re-activate the painful past, proclaim survival, and leave a tangible record to inspire filmmakers in the future. All of this speaks to Freda's immeasurable influence and legacy.

One of my first meetings at SBS Independent was with Rachel Perkins, whose dream was to make *Radiance*. This became the first Indigenous feature we supported. The film was shot by Warwick Thornton and it established Rachel as a filmmaker with a powerful creative voice. Freda's trainees now had their training wheels off and were on the way to being influencers themselves. Today, as we know, Erica,

Warwick and Rachel are leaders in their own right, forging new ground for Indigenous storytelling.

Freda – you have truly steered the boat, and your wide dynamic wake extends ever further, into second and third generations of filmmakers in your immediate family and your 'film family'.

You are the visionary matriarch with the powerful gaze and the canny wit ... selfless encourager, and helpful cajoler.

You are the pathfinder: to see it is to be it.

Margaret Pomeranz, AM,

hosted *The Movie Show* and *At the Movies* with David Stratton for 28 years and is currently co-hosting *Screen* on Foxtel with Graeme Blundell. She is past president of the Film Critics Circle of Australia and of Watch on Censorship. She is a board member of the Australian Film Institute and received the Adelaide Film Festival Don Dunstan Award, with David Stratton, in 2017.

from little things big things grow

Margaret Pomeranz, AM

I first met Warwick in 1998 when he was shooting *Radiance* with Rachel Perkins. That film revealed his cinematographer's eye. Just over ten years later I was asked to host a Q & A with Warwick at the Message Sticks Film Festival at the Sydney Opera House about a program of his short films. The year was 2009, the year of *Samson & Delilah*, which I had seen and which had overwhelmed me like no other Australian film had managed to do, with the possible exception of Peter Weir's *Gallipoli*. I was shaken. I remember interviewing Warwick at the Adelaide Film Festival that year and being overcome with tears during the interview. That was not something I do often in interviews.

So it was a joy for me to go back and look at the dramatic

films Warwick had made prior to his feature debut: *Payback*, *Mimi*, *Country Song*, *Nana* and *Green Bush*. There was an obvious strength and compassion in his approach to filmmaking, right from his earliest, *Payback*. There was an embrace of his Indigenous heritage in all of these films, mischievously in *Mimi*, affectionately in *Nana* and something else was there in *Green Bush*. That something was personal to Warwick. His story about the manning of a remote radio station was a story he knew well because he'd lived it.

Green Bush was the longest of the films and, both of us being smokers (which I'm loath to admit in public), we ducked out during the screening to suck foul air into our lungs. We came back to see the last, maybe ten minutes, of the film. Looking at the film on the monitor in the wings of the stage, I glanced at Warwick and was touched to see that he was really moved by his own film. By his own life up there on the screen. I don't often exploit that sort of situation but I was curious to know why he had been so affected by his own work. And then the story came out in front of the audience that the story of *Green Bush* was his own.

I believe Warwick is an emotional man who is able to channel that quality into his work so that we, the audience, not only get insight into his Indigenous world, we are able to connect empathetically, powerfully, with the stories he wants to share with us. It's actually a rare quality in a filmmaker, the ability to touch that emotional jugular.

Warwick is part of a vanguard of Indigenous filmmakers, along with his sister Erica Glynn, Rachel Perkins, Ivan Sen, Beck Cole and Wayne Blair, who have revolutionised our cinema by telling their stories in ways that have been embraced by wide audiences. So important and healing for this country as a whole.

The Message Sticks Festival was in early May that year. We already knew that *Samson & Delilah* had been selected for Un Certain Regard at the Cannes Film Festival, which was due to start a few days later. We all went for a drink afterwards, as you do, and I said then to Warwick that *Samson & Delilah* was going to win the Camera d'Or in Cannes. How prescient was I! But I'm not just boasting about being a know-all, it was a recognition that this, his debut feature, was the harbinger of a major talent on the world stage and if the jury in Cannes didn't recognise that then they had the wrong jury. And I had no idea what films *Samson & Delilah* would be up against. But anyone with a right mind could see the talent and the compassion embedded in the film. Some of the images from it will stay with me forever, particularly that smile on Delilah's face in the final scene.

Sweet Country premiered in competition at last year's Venice Film Festival and cemented Warwick's international reputation. I was lucky enough to be part of the post-screening dinner, just as the reviews were coming out from the three major international film publications: *Hollywood Reporter, Variety* and *Screen International.* It must be terrifying for a filmmaker to put their work up on the world stage where it will be dissected and judged. I had sat next to David Rooney from *Hollywood Reporter* during the screening, so I had a fair idea of how glowing his review would be. Sitting at the dinner table were those involved in the production. Their relief when his review came through on the net was palpable, the smile on Warwick's face a bit tentative. But to get the overwhelming endorsement from the other two publications was just mind-blowingly exciting. This was followed by the competition jury awarding *Sweet Country* the Special Jury Prize, an acknowledgement of just how much this filmmaker had achieved in his 20 years as a filmmaker.

It's been a privilege to witness his achievements. And to see this talent emerging in his son Dylan River just makes the future even brighter for Oz cinema. We can only be grateful to the Glynn family for spawning and nurturing their important talent.

David Stratton, AM,

is an author, film critic, lecturer and festival director who has served on the International Critics Jury in Cannes and on the Competition Jury in Venice. He is a recipient of the Raymond Longford Award and the Centenary Medal and was named Commander of the Ordre des Arts et des Lettres by the French Government.

standing ovation

David Stratton, AM

Two international film festivals – Cannes in 2009, Venice in 2017.

Samson & Delilah, Thornton's painfully honest film about an achingly vulnerable pair of Aboriginal star-crossed lovers, screens in the Un Certain Regard section at Cannes and the reception is rousing. A few days later, at the press video feed of the live TV coverage of the Closing Night celebrations, the president of the Camera D'Or (Best First Feature award) jury, French actor/director Roschdy Zem, is speaking (in French) about the film that has won this prestigious award. He's talking about a great love story, and even before he names the film I know he's talking about *Samson & Delilah*. What a triumph!

Eight years later I'm invited to be on the international jury in Venice. There are four actresses, four directors (one of them a woman) and me. The president is Annette Bening. Warwick's new film, *Sweet Country,* which I haven't seen, is one of the last films to be screened in competition. The standard of the films we've seen so far is unusually high: *Three Billboards Outside Ebbing Missouri* and *The Shape of Water* are among them, and there are also impressive films from Israel and Lebanon.

One morning at breakfast I see Warwick sitting alone at another table. Obviously I'm not allowed to discuss the work of the jury, but I join him for a coffee and try, as subtly as I can, to prepare him for the fact that the competition is extremely stiff. 'I'm relaxed. I know I've made a good film,' he says.

When we finally see *Sweet Country* I know he's right. It's one of the best Australian films since *Samson & Delilah.* When it ends there's an unusually lengthy standing ovation from the audience.

After the screening I'm invited to attend a dinner to celebrate the film. I sit next to Dylan, Warwick's son, who was responsible for the 2nd Unit photography. Everyone's excited, but I'm frustrated because I have to maintain a poker face and say nothing.

When the jury meets to discuss the films the debate is lively and opinionated. But I'm delighted to see that every jury member is impressed with Warwick's film to one degree or another. We decide to give it the Jury Prize, which is effectively the third prize (behind *The Shape of Water* and *Foxtrot*, the Israeli film).

At the closing ceremony the jury president assigns each member of the jury the task of presenting one of the awards. Annette asks me if I'd like to present Warwick's award. Of course I would. One of my proudest moments ever was giving the prize to this exceptional filmmaker on the stage of the Palazzo del Cinema.

Scott Hicks

an Emmy, Peabody and multiple AFI award-winning director, has also been nominated for Academy Awards for Best Director and Best Screenplay. His box-office sensation *Shine* was nominated for 7 Academy Awards including Best Film. Following a series of Hollywood studio films, Scott directed and shot the documentary feature *Glass: A Portrait of Philip in Twelve Parts*, which was short-listed for Oscar nomination and won the AFI Best Documentary Award.

(Photo: Stephen Laxton)

'real discovery lies not in seeking new landscapes, but in seeing with new eyes'

Scott Hicks

This quotation from Marcel Proust is engraved on a ring that I wear, a gift from my wife Kerry. A 20th-century French novelist may seem a remote reference for an Aboriginal Australian filmmaker, but his words in some way encapsulate my feelings about the work of Warwick Thornton. Director, writer and – does anyone deserve to be so talented? – a brilliant cinematographer as well, Warwick's storytelling has evolved a remarkable power all its own.

Much has been made in the annals of Australian cinema about the quality of the light, and the skills of generations of cinematographers in capturing the antediluvian landscapes of this continent, but I hazard the opinion that never has a cinematographer/director so clearly and meaningfully etched the essence of this country into his stories as Warwick Thornton.

From the simple, definitive image of white sugar dissolving into bubbling black water which opens *Sweet Country*, through to the absorption of the white man 'not right in the head', into the implacable landscape of the salt pan (a perfect counterpoint to David Lean's Lawrence emerging from the desert mirage), the true text of Warwick's films is delivered to us visually. These potent images transmit directly to our gut, beyond the ambiguity and banality of mere wordplay.

This affinity for visual communication seems to resonate with the documented feats of remarkable visual memory demonstrated by Aboriginal peoples, as well as the visual intelligence at work in the art of the tracker. The miniscule displacement of a leaf, a pebble, the graze of a foot or a hand in the dust – all things are there to be read by the observant Aboriginal eye.

Thornton's dark, knotty yet redemptive tales of human experience eloquently pass the test that I subjected TV movies to in my youth. By turning off the sound, I could assess whether their stories could be conveyed without words, or if they fell into that basket to which Alfred

Hitchcock contemptuously consigned most of American cinema: "as pictures of people talking."

Crystallised in Rowan McNamara's brilliant portrayal of Samson, the leading character who utters but a single word in the entire course of *Samson & Delilah*, Warwick reminds us that the real power of cinema is to tell us stories primarily through image. And etched in the DNA of his imagery is the archetypal struggle of black versus white, observed with unflinching gaze, without judgement, and in rigorously unsentimental fashion, together with the lightest of humorous touches that both ground his stories, and elevate them beyond polemic.

He has grasped the power of silence, together with that great rarity to be treasured: musical restraint. Never do you feel as if you are being manipulated towards an emotional response, as Warwick pays his audience the greatest respect in allowing them to make their own discoveries. And it is this astringency that lends his films their true emotional heft.

As with his use of silence rather than words, Warwick understands the power of darkness as much as light. His often rim-lit imagery, reminiscent of the almost lost art of the woodcut, touches the edges of Expressionism in its capacity to convey, wordlessly, profound and complex emotion.

This powerful restraint extends to his command of performance. It reminds me that some of the richest of my earliest experiences in the world of filmmaking intersected with that other Aboriginal genius of Australian cinema, David Gulpilil, perhaps our greatest screen actor. As a lowly crew member on *Storm Boy* and later on *The Last Wave*, I had the extraordinary opportunity to observe at close quarters a talent akin to that which I've been trying to define in Warwick.

Gulpilil has always displayed an instinctive understanding that the art of great cinema performance is rooted in simply *being* in front of the camera. As one great actor put it to me, it's the ability to do nothing, but to do it extremely well. So Gulpilil's face can occupy the entire screen at the end of *Charlie's Country*, with no emotional display or actorly devices. In doing so, his countenance completely absorbs us, capturing our attention for minutes on end. We scrutinise its landscape, its clefts and ravines etched by experience, the gaze of his eyes fixed on an unseen horizon beyond the immediate world. Entirely visual. Without words. Still.

On the night of the premiere of *Sweet Country* in Adelaide, Warwick remarked that the main character in the film is the landscape itself. That aside, all of the performances in the film are excellent – and this does not happen by chance. When you work with a cast of actors with vastly different experiences, one of the director's tasks is to ensure that everyone is acting in the same film. Warwick's direction achieves this with deceptive ease and characteristic humility.

Now, I'm not blind to the irony of an aging Anglophone white guy like me holding forth on the power of the Aboriginal voice. But somewhere in all of this there does lie a lesson for the rest of us. To me, Warwick's art affords us a glimpse of a world beyond the hooting and hollering of much of our screen storytelling. He conveys an instinctive understanding of the power that lies beyond words, to where a flickering shadow on a wall can express more than all the words and music and visual effects that we've come to rely on.

Importantly, it's the unique vision of Warwick Thornton that points a way through the seemingly impenetrable jungle we confront as we struggle to make sense of our experience, our history, our presence on this continent whose edges we cling to.

Without this clarity of vision, this ability to tell important stories with power and grace, we can only echo the despairing words uttered by Sam Neill's character Fred Smith in *Sweet Country*: 'What chance has this country got?'

In 1995, **Maryanne Redpath** started work at the Berlin International Film Festival and in 2008 became head of the Generation section, which screens extraordinary art-house and world cinema for young people. She is festival delegate for Australia and New Zealand and head curator of the Berlinale Special Series *NATIVe – A Journey into Indigenous Cinema.*

gathering power

Maryanne Redpath

Dear Erica,

I think we first met many years ago in the early 2000s over oysters and beer in a bar somewhere. It was a meeting with the Indigenous Department of the AFC. I was on my annual film-scouting tour, travel-weary and ready to go home, but I could not refuse this wonderful opportunity to get to know the key figures behind a blossoming part of the Australian film industry, of which I had only a little knowledge – and a heap of curiosity.

Over the years it became our tradition; getting together for a big catch-up. Exciting, inspirational, political and personal at the same time, we discussed everything and I got to ask questions – and to listen. You are a great teacher and I am honoured to learn from you.

I have always been aware of your presence at these get-togethers. Although you never put yourself front and centre, your presence was commanding, uncompromising, at the same time curious and with a healthy dose of scepticism. Your mission: to carry forth Freda Glynn's work, and that of her collaborators and of CAAMA, for self-empowerment and entertainment through the exploration, enabling and realisation of cinematic storytelling of Indigenous Australians.

Your advice for Berlinale NATIVe proved invaluable: you gave us backbone and allowed us to ask sticky questions.

In 2011 our journeys intersected at the World Indigenous Cinema Conference at Kautokeino, in Sápmi in icy northern Norway. It was freezing, we laughed a lot and ate reindeer meat together. You gave an enlightening keynote address on cinema, language, country – and the ownership of story. You began by apologising that where you come from people swear a lot, which reminded me of something else you'd once said: 'They're our fucking stories and we're going to fucking tell them!'

These words are the truth, they are authentically you. Necessary and blatantly clear. Please, insist on telling those stories for big screens everywhere. Apologies for swearing not accepted.

In March 2018 I attended the second World Indigenous Cinema Conference. Many Indigenous filmmakers and institutional representatives travelled across the globe to be there. You would have been as amazed and proud as I was to see what has developed on a global and regional level over the last seven years. I missed sharing reindeer meat with you.

From those modest beginnings, it has become obvious that a mighty tsunami of Indigenous cinema is gathering power, and it's due to come crashing down on the world.

Erica, you are a driving force with your presence, your strength and guidance, your boldness, the twinkle in your eye, your calling a spade a spade, your humanity, your skilful filmmaking. Without you, and the collective legacy of your mother, of CAAMA, this tsunami would be a sorry little wave.

Dear Warwick,
Through your visionary sense of cinema, your masterful storytelling, your artistry and eye for detail, your connection to self and to your origins, you have opened doors onto multi-layered worlds where reality is suspended.

You have created space for other often painful realities. You take story, rhythm and image firmly into your possession and invite viewers into those worlds.

When *Green Bush* was screened at the Berlin Film Festival I was happy to meet you properly. The film won the Panorama Short Film award and I remember being enchanted by your gratitude and humility at being discovered in this context. You made the film, I thought; I was just the messenger. *Green Bush* is seminal: bush radio, great music, messages for the incarcerated and always a good 'cuppa tea' to be brewed – a phrase which became a team-slogan in Berlin when we needed time-out.

And then you hit us with your first feature film – the masterfully sensitive and furious award-winning *Samson & Delilah*. A whole bunch of hardened festival curators were simply blown away.

At the first Berlinale NATIVe, your presence was inimitable. Your support gave us backbone and helped keep the work on track. It was around that time that I learned that you and Erica share the same mother. And when you also called me 'sis', I felt so blessed!

As fate would have it, our paths re-connected at the multi-site art exhibition dOCUMENTA (13), in Kassel, Germany. I stumbled across a dusty, travel-worn van parked in front of an art gallery. A video screen in the back portrayed an elder woman, an artist, sitting on the ground painting and next to her a boy, learning. *Mother Courage.* First I suspected, then I determined, that this was your installation, to be parked in front of a different gallery every other day. It was transcendent – in your physical absence you were (collectively) omnipresent.

I remember a journalist asking you in Berlin: 'Who exactly is Indigenous?' and you answered, 'We're all Indigenous, you only have to look back far enough.' Generous answer I thought. Went down well with the Germans.

We sometimes talked about the difficulty of getting your second feature film up after the successes of *Samson & Delilah*. The pressure was on. You were so prolific, trying your hand at different formats, success measured on other scales, and then boom! Along you came with the incredibly powerful *Sweet Country*, to national and international acclaim. Respect!

Dear Freda Glynn,
We have never met but our paths have crossed many times and I am well aware of your work being carried on by your children and your grandchildren. Thank you for CAAMA,

for your dedication to being prophetic and an advocator and for building the inspirational foundations for the cinematic storytelling of the Aboriginal and Torres Straits Peoples. Your legacy is in excellent hands.

With love, peace and respect,

Maryanne

Penny Smallacombe

is a Maramanindji woman from the Northern Territory. She is Head of Indigenous at Screen Australia, a former senior programmer for NITV, and an experienced documentary producer and director. She has a Masters of Arts in Documentary Producing from AFTRS, and started her career at the ABC with a producing cadetship. She produced numerous documentaries for the long-running *Message Stick* series. Other credits include *Yarning Up* (series 1 & 2), *A Change of Heart*, and a series of shorts titled *The Forgotten Ones*.

excellence

Penny Smallacombe

I've avoided writing this piece, not because I don't think the Glynn family are exceptional, but rather I am terrified I won't be able to summarise just how extraordinary I think they are! As far as family legacies go, the Glynn/Thornton/River family have contributed to the Australian screen industry in ways audiences will continue to discuss and learn about for many years to come. This is by no means an exaggeration. Future AFTRS, VCA and students at other film schools within Australia and possibly overseas will learn how a movement began when Freda pioneered Indigenous broadcasting in Central Australia, and about the body of work left behind by Erica Glynn, Warwick Thornton, Dylan River and Tanith Glynn-Maloney. Who knows what kind of stories Tanith and Dylan's kids might end up making. They will of course read this and think, Christ, that Penny, she can really talk shit! And that is also the kind of down-to-earth legacy-holding family they are!

As a younger, want-to-be producer, Erica use to scare the hell out of me! She has a commanding tone, and an instinct for story like no other. I know she was unsure of me. I'd failed in my attempts to get not one but two NIDF docos from development and into production. But still she and Sally Riley (the dynamic duo) took a chance on me and I was selected for the Indigenous Producers Initiative. It was then and there I saw the nurturing side of Erica. Don't worry, I was still scared, but I knew I wanted to learn from her. Fast forward ten years, and I found myself sitting in a pub with her while she explained this new documentary initiative about working with remote communities to help them record and make short docos about songlines. It won't be easy, she said, someone will have to navigate the secret and sacred nature of songlines, and NITV will need a broadcast outcome at the same time ... She then asked, 'We need someone to oversee this, do you have any thoughts?' I said, me! Take me! And so it began, I left NITV and jumped headfirst into the Indigenous Department at Screen Australia to work with Erica and the rest of the team. It was absolutely by stealth she got me there. A true strategist is Erica. A year later Erica's time at Screen Australia was quickly coming to an end. I had started taking detailed notes of everything she said about story, or how to speak to a filmmaker about their project. There was definitely panic at the thought of not having daily access to her wisdom, experience and advice. And of course the note-taking completely freaked her out. I doubt she truly knows how brilliant she really is!

When Erica handed the reins to me as the new head of the Indigenous Department it was stressful and exciting. How on earth was I going to fill her shoes? Excellence ... she kept repeating the word 'excellence' to me. 'Everything we fund has to be excellent.' Excellent stories, excellent filmmakers, we have to provide excellent professional development opportunities ... *excellence*!' Four-and-a-half years on, it only now makes sense. The legacy of the Indigenous Department is built on excellence and the work of Erica Glynn and the other departmental heads. It's not easy nurturing young filmmakers through this industry. Helping them find their own authentic voice. Watching them stumble around in the dark until they find a narrative through line! You have to say no to funding filmmakers more than you get to say yes. Sometimes you feel like a dream slayer. But you keep ploughing and you keep supporting and eventually magic is made. Erica has helped create a lot of magic and the success the department has today is a testament to her, and the many years she spent building the Indigenous screen industry.

It is hard to build a screen industry; it's just as bloody hard to create an authentic screen experience that speaks loudly to people. Warwick makes quiet films that yell. How on earth someone makes almost-silent films that yell is beyond me. But he does. Like Erica, Warwick works by stealth. He sneaks you into an intimate world (for most audiences a world far removed from their own), settles you in for the ride and then punches you in the guts several times over. And somehow you come out feeling all the more better for the experience. *Samson & Delilah. Sweet Country.* Incredible!

I knew *Sweet Country* was going to be good. David Tranter and Steven McGregor had created a fantastic script. Warwick had come on board and before the shoot he talked about a few scenes that really made me think this film is going to be exceptional. We are all there at the rough cut. Comfy seats, Gold Class in Moore Park. Slightly stressed looking producers in David and Greer, and a super relaxed looking Warwick. All on board for an early morning screening. It was incredible. Brilliant! Mostly quiet, mostly yells. That was *Sweet Country*. Developed over years, shot in 21 days, and remembered forever. And I'll remember the five-minute standing ovation at Venice Film Festival for its world premiere. That's what excellence feels like.

I'll let you into a little secret most people don't know about blackfellas, *nothing comes easy*! I worry that when future film school students look back at this family legacy, and think that building the foundation for the Central Australian Aboriginal Media Association was easy for Freda. That shooting and directing well over twenty 30-minute language documentaries and several award-winning shorts before winning a Camera D'Or for *Samson & Delilah* was easy for Wok. That working in a government department to hold the hands of many Indigenous screen practitioners through their first, second and third filmmaking adventures was easy for Erica. Trust me, it's not. Breaking new ground never is. But still they did it, and so future film school students, think about that, about how difficult this journey has been for each of them. Bloody legends!

Creating a legacy sounds exhausting if you ask me.

Lisa Stefanoff

is an anthropologist, curator, media producer and writer who has lived in the NT and worked with local filmmakers and artists for over 15 years. She worked and conducted PhD research at CAAMA from 2002–2006. A graduate of the New York University Department of Anthropology Program in Culture and Media, she is currently an ARC research fellow at the National Institute for Experimental Arts, UNSW Art & Design, and honorary research associate at Charles Darwin University School of Creative Arts and Humanities.

CAAMA and the art of mediating desert cultural survivance

Lisa Stefanoff

One of the stories that can be told about CAAMA is a story about Central Australian Aboriginal media activism and innovation as a moment in a long tradition and history of desert women's committed care for country, family, language and culture. Freda Glynn, a visionary Kaytetye woman, became a cultural figurehead and impressive role model through her work to empower Aboriginal people to control broadcast media and the stories it could tell about them and their worlds. Co-creating a regional Aboriginal media service was a massive undertaking given the social and cultural complexity of the vast desert area called 'Central Australia'. Bringing CAAMA into being involved bringing together people from many language groups with shared but different histories, needs and aspirations. Freda did this feisty and demanding work also as a mother growing up five children, in a town riven with the social scars of frontier 'settlement'. Freda worked, of course, in close co-operation with many people to build CAAMA and to establish Imparja Television but her living legacy – two further directly related generations of award-winning Aboriginal media-makers walking the path she opened – is unique and significant. Although by no means representative of the entirety of the many tales that could be told as 'the CAAMA story', the overlapping careers of three generations of the Glynn family – Freda, her filmmaker children Erica, Warwick and grandchildren Tanith Glynn-Maloney and Dylan River, her CAAMA Radio producer son Robbie, and occasional actor son Scott – are iconic of this determined creation and transmission of a new Central Australian Aboriginal cultural tradition through family lines and within community. Looking laterally, Freda's daughters-in-law Penelope McDonald and Beck Cole have also played significant roles in this lineage, both as filmmakers and as family relations.

Freda and her early CAAMA colleagues created a home for Aboriginal people, voices and dreams to work together. The impacts of the efforts of early CAAMA mob are diverse and far-reaching, from Alice Springs to Hollywood. Warwick Thornton and fellow acclaimed Central Australian Aboriginal filmmaker Rachel Perkins were recently invited to join the American Academy of Motion Pictures, Arts and Sciences, the organisation that annually awards the Oscars. Rachel and Warwick began working at CAAMA in the 1980s, as teenagers, along with Erica Glynn, Robbie Thornton and many others. Probably no one quite imagined that recording old people's stories under trees in the baking heat, lighting night shots with fires and car headlights and connecting more deeply through this kind of work with family living on country would carry the young trainees to the table of the world's most prestigious guild of cinema practitioner-judges. The founding spirit of CAAMA and immersion in an entirely unique organically emerging, socially organised and culturally imprinted mode of DIY media production did however infuse a restless fin-de-siècle generation of Aboriginal screen storytellers with a solid confidence that their time was *the* time for Aboriginal media, stories and voices from Aboriginal country to start to take their rightful place in the world. It was high time for Indigenous media to shake things up, at home and abroad, and CAAMA was a lightning rod for energetic people to stir the pot.

CAAMA, the Central Australian Aboriginal Media Association, emerged as a desert expression of late 1970s Australian Aboriginal self-determination politics. As CAAMA co-founder Philip Batty described earlier in this volume, Central Australian (post)colonial intercultural social dynamics, a relatively progressive Aboriginal policy environment, Indigenous media forays in Canada and elsewhere, and a fast expanding set of accessible media production and broadcasting technologies all shaped CAAMA as a regional, town-based, Aboriginal media foundry. The first CAAMA Television news and current affairs program *Urrpeye* (*Messenger*) was produced by the organisation's first group of trainees, learning their craft on the job from Philip Batty's brother David (filmmaker legend in his own right, perhaps best known for *Bush Mechanics*, the series he made with Warlpiri Media friends in the 1990s). When CAAMA Television was coming into being, David was working as the 'audio-visual technician' of the Alice Springs 'Education Centre', managing the only video gear then in the desert, sending it to communities to shoot small story segments for a program he would compile in town called *The Look Show*. Under the maternal guidance of Freda in the 1980s and her successors in the 1990s, CAAMA attracted and cultivated a younger 'second-generation' cohort of Aboriginal screen media-makers – Warwick, Erica, Rachel, Trisha Morton-Thomas, Cilla Collins, Allan Collins, David Tranter, Steven McGregor, Jason Ramp, Beck Cole, Danielle MacLean, Mitch Torres, Robyn Nardoo, and Dena Curtis, in particular – who have shaped not only Australian Indigenous media as we know it, but national cinema more broadly. Many of this cohort grew up in Alice Springs. Those who didn't were connected to the desert from all directions, from Broome, Darwin and South Australia.

CAAMA has always concurrently made media *and* media-makers. Within 30 years of the first arrival of VHS cameras and editing technology in the desert, CAAMA Production's distinctive cultural commitments, production ethics and identity in the Australian screen/media industries moved into the hands of a 'third generation' of strong and talented media artists who call the desert home. Like their parents, they have no problem assembling top industry talent from the cities into relatively small, sharp operating crews. Recent award-winning films such as Dylan River's *Nulla Nulla* and *Buckskin* embody the inheritance of an empowering spirit of cultural reinvention with multi-genre screen-based story-telling at its heart.

Like many other persisting Central Australian Aboriginal organisations that emerged around the same time, CAAMA stands today as a symbol of a time in Australian history when the stars of decolonising politics, non-Aboriginal solidarity, community strength, government policy, and tenacious visionary leadership aligned to institutionalise a means of producing and amplifying Aboriginal voices as powerful and enduring presences in the public sphere. The ferment of politics, passion, vision, determination, creativity and intercultural tactics and collaboration at the heart of CAAMA has, since its earliest days, converted extensive desert histories of loss, marginalisation, disempowerment, inaudibility and invisibility into exemplary and ongoing nation-jolting practices of vocal, assured, future-reaching cultural 'survivance' (to borrow a term from Native American scholar Gerald Vizenor).

Beyond the patronage of the state, the machinations of the screen industry and the talent and creativity of individual story-makers, the magic of this cultural alchemy, that turns the dispossessions of European 'settlement' into rare earth crystals of communication to the world, lies in a powerful mix of necessity, perception, imagination, pain, love, care, respect, humour, creativity, grit and tremendous generosity.

The birth of CAAMA Radio 8-KIN FM was revolutionary.

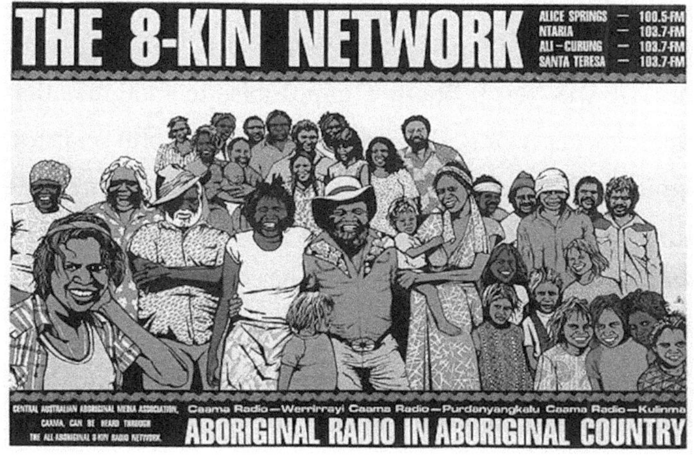

'The 8-Kin Network', designed by Michael Callaghan and Ray Young, Redback Graphix, 1985. (Reproduced courtesy of CAAMA.)

In the late 1970s, Aboriginal people in Alice Springs rarely saw or heard themselves represented positively in any media and couldn't listen to their own languages, stories or songs on radio. Freda Glynn, along with comrades-in-arms Phillip Batty, John Macumba and many others, sought to change this, forever. Their dream was for Central Australian Aboriginal people to make, listen to and watch stories, songs, news, community service announcements, education programs made by and for Aboriginal people, in their own languages, in their own country. By taking control of recording, editing and broadcast technologies desert people could, in the words of their Warlpiri friend and colleague Francis Jupurrurla Kelly, 'fight fire with fire'. It was hard, but not impossible, to imagine, that one day, carrying the sparks of this pivotal cultural ignition, Aboriginal filmmaker role models might grace international red carpets, install video works in Europe's leading contemporary art events, be coveted as subjects for the nation's most prestigious portrait prize, and lend their vote to Hollywood's definitive competition for global screen industry recognition and value.

CAAMA is a resoundingly Alice Springs institution and would not be the same place had it been established elsewhere. Now standing physically just off one of the main inner intersections of the desert town, not far from the Town Council, its dusty sunset-pink façade faces west, a bank of windows reflecting the dipping golden light of Central and Western Arrernte country every afternoon. Before occupying this prominent position directly across from what was for years a busy bar and accommodation complex, and backing onto the usually dry ancient Todd River, CAAMA was a set of 'demountables' on the edge of the lively Little Sisters (Inarlange) town camp on the southern outskirts of town. In Warwick Thornton's breakthrough short drama *Greenbush* (2005), based on his own early

CAAMA Radio days, DJ Kenny looks after families seeking refuge in the studio building when troubles outside become too wild or unpredictable, as they often did.

When Freda Glynn was raising her five children in Alice Springs and working tirelessly to ensure that CAAMA survived, racism was rife in public culture and still institutionally entrenched. Poverty, ill health, homelessness, grogging, social and state violence, boredom and other modes of precarity equally coloured young people's experiences, perceptions and fears, and fuelled passionate desires for empowerment and change. The frontier town's population expanded in the 1980s as the zeitgeist of self-determination breathed vision and purpose into a range of local organisations to manage Aboriginal people's interests, from land rights to health care, law to community management, education to broadcasting. Political activists, cultural researchers, social justice-inclined professionals started to flow in from 'down south'. They and a sizeable US spy base population grew steadily alongside long-standing local Aboriginal, Afghan, European and mixed-heritage families living in town and in its fringe camps. Idealistic teachers and lawyers, artists, ringers, linguists, anthropologists, journalists, nurses, church workers, lesbian peace activists, drifting musicians, mad inventors, grog runners, career Commonwealth and NT public servants, earth scientists, and all manner of tradies made themselves at home in Alice and thickened the town's eddies of social engagement, commercial exploitation and cultural experimentation. Tourism expanded, drawing in more and more people wanting to 'experience Aboriginal culture' in some way. The education system struggled to hold students through their high school years. Many kids dreamed of careers in sport. Some learned early about the rules and rough edges of whitefella law, while others left town in the hot summers to learn their Law/Lore and returned with new status and the challenge of maintaining relationship to country while finding their way, a good way, of being off country permanently or for stretches of time. The hand back of Uluru to its traditional owners in 1985 put desert Australia into a new place in imaginations on all sides of politics, all over the world.

The birth of self-determined media in Alice Springs happened more or less concurrently with similar moves in the southern and western desert settlements of Ernabella (Pukatja) and Yuendumu, where Pitjantjatjara and Warlpiri media emerged through EVTV and the Warlpiri Media Association. CAAMA was, and arguably has remained, as much an atelier for making Aboriginal media and Aboriginal media-makers as an experiment in Aboriginal representation drawing together the voices, histories, contemporary struggles and future visions of multiple desert cultural groups. Although located in and centred in many ways by the forces of desert worlds, CAAMA also drew in Aboriginal people from communities, towns and cities nationwide, as well as whitefellas from many places. From the start, families, peer groups, and kin networks formed strong cohorts within and in relationship to the organisation. With the exception of the desert music world of largely male bands that moved through CAAMA Music studios, women and men were equally at home and represented in all areas of production and management.

CAAMA's storytelling on screen has always been rooted deeply and equally in Aboriginal people's contemporary circumstances and struggles and the practices and protocols of its filmmakers' elders and ancestors. As a contemporary practice of public Aboriginality, CAAMA media has also manifested the will of a progressive seam of Australian cultural politics and its institutionally empowered and more radical autonomous supporters and purveyors. Aboriginal Affairs, Arts and Culture ministers and senior bureaucrats under Gough Whitlam, Don Dunstan and others during the 1970s gave this politics breathing space through an array of policy initiatives and emergent art and culture research, collecting and training institutions including the Australian Institute for Aboriginal and Torres Strait Islander Studies (AIATSIS), the Australian Film, Television, and Radio School (AFTRS) and the Australian Film Commission (AFC, now Screen Australia). Over time, CAAMA built formative relationships with, or undertook projects, training and production initiatives with, these national bodies. CAAMA's new mode of claiming presence in the local, regional and eventually national mediascape generated its own momentum from the end of the 1970s, supported by visionary colleagues at the ABC and later, in the 1980s and 1990s, also by SBS. Most significantly in the first decade of its existence, CAAMA was instrumental in the establishment of the first Aboriginal-owned-and-controlled commercial television broadcasting station, Imparja Television. The sale of early desert paintings, artefacts, and music cassettes through the CAAMA Shop further established CAAMA as a key point of distribution of desert Aboriginal artistry, voice and cultural power.

Warwick and Erica and their three other siblings Susan, Scott and Robert grew up in Alice Springs in the 1970s and 80s as part of a local generation of 'townies' who heard Arrernte, Warlpiri, Anmatyerre, Alywarr, Warumungu,

Luritja, Pintupi, Pitjantjatjara and other of the vast central desert's ancient languages around them in town every day, learning a little, while speaking English as their own first language. Emplacement in town was a mode of displacement from the time and space of their ancestral origins. They grew up with senses of both proximity to and distance from their cultural heritage and birthright. Freda's Kaytetye country north of Alice Springs had borne the brunt of colonial frontier violence hard: killings, theft of land and water, removal of children, and the violent bondage labour indenture had deep impacts. Entrenched forms of racism lingered in the area and despite criss-crossing histories of kindness and friendship from some quarters of the settler population, racialised tensions coloured the energy of their home town.

In the 1980s, town kids had to make their own fun, find their own ways of being both teenaged and Aboriginal in a place etched deeply with old power dynamics and emerging cultural challenges, as new waves of whitefellas, new social services, new forms of commercial life, new addictions and new opportunities started to pull people from remote communities into and out of town in ever greater numbers. Like all teenagers, they had to somehow create their own meaningful pathways in a heady, socially complex world not of their own creation.

Films were only available at the drive-in or at 'walk-in' cinema, or later on VCR. Westerns were extremely popular, the ambivalence of cowboy or Indian identification for people with cattle station histories and working lives notwithstanding. Westerns showed Indian country panoramically and the spacious beauty full of drama resonated deeply. No commercial television broadcasting reached the central desert in the early 1980s. Certainly no dedicated national Indigenous television service shared Indigenous media with the nation on a daily basis as it does today. Unlike teenagers' lives elsewhere in the country, mass Euro-Australian/American televisual pop culture wasn't naturalised as a primary architecture of identification or fantasy. Music – on radio, LP or cassette, and on *Countdown* on ABC TV – carried a lot of this cultural load. They knew the pleasure and power of looking at the inkiest starriest sky from a swag beside a hard-wood fire, listening to the bush or a Johnny Cash album, or both. Relatively untethered from the pop culture anchors of 1980s teenage mainstream Australia, Alice Springs Aboriginal town kids' identities were perhaps a more open set of possibilities than either their bush cousins or faraway non-Aboriginal city folk.

If teenaged Warwick was, by day, spending time throwing red rocks at girls to get their attention (as he has often recalled when talking about the listless energy of young desert men like Samson the protagonist of his multi-award-winning feature film *Samson & Delilah*, 2009), he was, like *Greenbush*'s Kenny, also spinning vinyl on CAAMA Radio, sending song requests to prisoners from their family, playing pre-recorded community service messages in local languages on analogue tape 'cart' technology. At the same time, Erica was being trained (alongside Rachel Perkins, Rachel Wellington and David Renahan, and others) to produce video current affairs, culture and history stories for the fledgling CAAMA Television Unit. Friends David Tranter, Allan Collins, Steven McGregor and Priscilla Collins soon joined the Film and Television – 'Productions' – cohort. In video news, current affairs and documentary work in particular they were mixing with relations and other people from all over the desert, and beyond, learning about the powers of storytelling to connect people intimately and at a distance, learning how to mediate between bush and town worlds. Elsewhere at CAAMA, other friends found roles in the CAAMA Radio and Music studios where desert rock bands pushed 11s on their Marshall amps in the music studios. Big town gigs like 'Rock Against Racism' and 'Rock Without Grog' (that have since become legendary events) and Midnight Oil tours drew crowds to town from all over the desert. The Warumpi Band, Coloured Stone, No Fixed Address, Lajamanu Teenage Band, to name only a few, packed out local gigs. Aboriginal country music players like Issac Yamma and Gus Williams deepened their own traditions, paving the way for their sons Frankie Yamma and Warren H. Williams o step into the limelight as young adults, and African–American activists visited CAAMA offering solidarity in the struggle and, sometimes, some cash. At the same time Freda was, with Philip, John and others, pulling together the vision of an Aboriginal-controlled television licence in defiance of the prospect of a 'bombardment' of non-Aboriginal content raining down from the impending launch of the AUSSAT satellite.

CAAMA strengthened its position in the local cultural landscape alongside the growth of sister organisations such as the Central Land Council (CLC), the Institute for Aboriginal Development (IAD), Tangentyere Council, Ngaanyatjarra Pitjantjatjara Yankunytjatjara (NPY) Women's Council, the Central Australian Aboriginal Legal Aid Service (CAALAS), the Central Australian Aboriginal Congress (CAAC) health service, Yipirinya school, and other organisations. Against the grain of identifications of traditional ownership and stewardship and the cartographical delineations of country that became the focus of land rights and native title struggles, CAAMA emerged and grew as a genuinely open social enterprise, a space in which traditional and emerging networks of connection between people would inform new and distinctive modes of cultural production.

CAAMA's collective push to keep language and culture strong through media production and broadcasting was intergenerational and culturally diverse from the start. Language speakers in CAAMA's Language Services Department guided the research and creative work of those who spoke only, or mostly, English.

Grounded in traditional economies and generational hierarchies of holding and sharing, CAAMA's screen work has always prioritised respectful listening as the primary mode of engagement with 'bush' storytellers and their tales. CAAMA Productions' long-running language and culture 'maintenance and preservation' documentary series *Nganampa Anwernekenhe* ('Ours' in Pitjantjatjara and Arrernte languages), produced originally exclusively for Imparja Television and later in production collaboration with ABC TV and SBS/NITV, exemplified this aesthetic. *Nganampa*s mediated bush voices and stories for local and distant audiences, and their makers became adept at this work of cultural translation.

For years after he completed his BA degree at AFTRS, Warwick Thornton honed his cinematographic, storytelling and directorial skills and his poetic apprehension of desert lives in part through regular *Nganampa* development and production. As he conjured his career as a feature film director, the *Nganampa* ethics and aesthetics of 'listening to old fellas sitting under trees telling stories' informed his approaches to dramatic desert Aboriginal screen storytelling, especially inasmuch as the latter came to involve 'untrained' local actors/storytellers. Working with his photo-media artist friend Michael Riley also had a great impact and an aesthetics of stillness came into greater focus in his own work. Documentary and dramatic narratives told slowly, with sparse dialogue and full of the stillness of sitting, waiting and anticipating, based on true stories, shot on country and in this groundedness evoking the presence and power of ancestral forces became what is now an unmistakeable signature visual and directorial style.

* * *

Since the birth of CAAMA, thousands of Aboriginal people and non-Aboriginal collaborators have contributed to hundreds of music, radio, film/video, television and online media projects that have occupied thousands of Australian broadcast hours and garnered scores of awards. CAAMA's large archive of films and videos, music recordings, radio programs and community service media has rightly been recognised internationally as a pivotal force in the preservation, maintenance and promotion of desert Aboriginal language and culture. Its value lies not only in its rare documentation of endangered languages, traditional knowledge and regional history but in the distinctive mode of production of this rich 'content', based always on protocols for doing things the right way in Aboriginal country.

Documentary and drama films made by past and present CAAMA mob speak many languages. They have soared to the pinnacles of national and international industries and reached audiences in every corner of the globe because they tell Aboriginal stories from a firm and proper footing in Aboriginal worlds. Every frame, every line of dialogue and every cut enfolds storytelling protocols. These may be invisible to the eyes and ears of some audiences but they sit at the heart of the films' truth and power. The films and their makers have shown the world that mixing desert cultural practices of dwelling in and looking after country, respectful listening, dramatic storytelling, intergenerational creativity with a political will to represent a broad spectrum of ways of being Aboriginal in the 20th and 21st centuries precipitates a rare cultural alchemy.

The Central Australian Aboriginal Media Association was founded on and has been for almost 40 years a key site of what philosopher Jonathan Lear (2006) calls 'radical hope'. As one of the key torchbearers of this forward-looking forward-pushing force against the devastations of colonisation, Freda Glynn occupies a special place in Australian cultural history and will long be recognised as a pioneering desert Aboriginal woman. CAAMA is the ground out of which the country's most successful Indigenous media talent has grown; a group of storytellers with an abiding commitment to cultural survival as an artful undertaking. Their screen-making work keeps their cultural identities strong by working closely with people living on country to share their stories and languages with distant audiences. It carries the past into the future. Radical hope becomes survivance. Alongside many other talented Australian Indigenous filmmakers, Freda Glynn's children and grandchildren will undoubtedly continue to craft some of the world's most powerful and necessary screen culture. With any luck so too will their children. And theirs. And theirs. Viva CAAMA!

I thank many people in the CAAMA community for sharing their stories and day-to-day lives with me over the years (2002–2006) I worked alongside them as an anthropologist, and in the roles of CAAMA Productions Production Assistant, Production Manager, and Distribution Manager.

Wayne Blair

is a Batjala Waka Waka man and an acclaimed film, television and theatre director, writer, actor and producer. His feature film directing credits include *Top End Wedding* and *The Sapphires*, and for television *Cleverman* and *Redfern Now*, in which he also acted. He has been awarded the Bob Maza Fellowship by Screen Australia, the Andrew Myer Fellowship by the Australian Film, Television and Radio School, and the Richard Wherrett Fellowship by the Sydney Theatre Company.

Freda

Wayne Blair

I arrived in Sydney in 1999 and through my work I made this city my base. My original training was as an actor; I received an opportunity to write and direct my first short film via Uncle Lester Bostock and Metro Screen. Uncle Lester said I should get Warwick Thornton to be the cinematographer. This moment was the beginning of our friendship.

Over the past couple of decades I have met his family and have worked directly with Nana Freda, Erica, Dylan and Tanith. All of them have welcomed me into their world and family.

Nana Freda is the spear point of the family that I know. I feel fortunate to have met her and I've benefited from her hard work as a champion for blackfella filmmakers, and filmmakers alike. Freda, and many others like my own nana and mum, have sacrificed a great deal for what we now possess.

She (they) gave me opportunity.

Confidence.

Self-esteem.

Courage.

Pride.

I am so glad I met Warwick, my brother, back in the last century.

This whole family continues to tell our stories with artistic brilliance while maintaining that humility. (Maybe except for Dylan and his Instagram account.) I am honoured to write this and to have known them in my lifetime.

With warmth,

Wayne Blair

Liam Egan

has made a living out of sound for over 30 years and has more than 40 Australian and international feature film credits as sound designer/sound supervisor. He has also worked in television drama and documentary, and has been the sound designer on many non-film projects, ranging from interactive and full dome to multimedia and virtual reality.

35,000 feet away

Liam Egan

There are times in my life when I have looked back on the important milestones, those moments when things started or ended, moments that didn't seem significant at the time but with the benefit of hindsight were monumental and life changing. I had such an experience one day back in 1989. On that day I met, in quick succession, Freda Glynn, Erica Glynn and Warwick Thornton.

I had travelled to Alice Springs to teach sound recording to the current intake of trainees at the CAAMA (Central Australian Aboriginal Media Association) television unit. I went with John Whitteron and Tony Stephens, who were there to teach cinematography and editing, respectively.

On our first teaching day, John, Tony and I drove to

CAAMA and met up with Freda Glynn, who was to be our boss for the time we were there. CAAMA Radio had been an exciting and successful venture for about a decade by that time, and Imparja TV had recently been launched in Alice Springs, with a big shiny new building. CAAMA was the brainchild of Freda Glynn, Phillip Batty and John Macumba, but Freda ran it. Freda spoke quietly but she was clearly the one in charge. Freda inducted us and conducted a tour of the CAAMA building. We were to be based in the shed-like CAAMA TV soundstage.

While we were having our tour a film crew returned to CAAMA in a 4WD Toyota and started to unpack their gear. A young woman holding a clipboard came over to Freda and started talking to her. I thought she was very beautiful and so cool! I'm sure I remember her wearing a black-leather jacket but now, as I think back, it would seem an impractical wardrobe choice for a filmmaker out on a shoot in Central Australia.

Freda introduced her to us as Erica, her daughter, a trainee in an earlier intake she was now working for CAAMA as a producer. Erica was polite but basically took no interest in us. Warwick told me years later that, at the time, she was making a documentary about the artist Emily Kngwarreye, long before she became world famous.

From that point on, although I saw her at a distance (did I mention how cool she was?), our paths at CAAMA hardly crossed.

Finally, on that day, we were to meet the current crop of trainees we would be teaching. That is when I met Warwick Thornton. I remember being introduced to the group and being struck by how shy they all seemed. The trainees I remember the clearest were Warwick (who I knew was Freda's son), Jason (whose surname is lost to me in the mists of time but who I think was from Tasmania), and Rachel Perkins (who I vaguely knew because she went to school with my younger brother in Canberra).

It became pretty clear early on that the trainees were only interested in learning about the camera, although some were interested in editing. None of them were very interested in sound recording. And it became clear that access to the cameras was down to whoever got in first. My memory tells me that this was usually Warwick and Jason, and they didn't do any sound recording.

The equipment we had to work with was basic. At the time they were shooting on U-matic portapaks, which consisted of a ¾-inch video recorder carried over the shoulder with a video camera connected to it. Sound was recorded on a Nagra reel-to-reel recorder (weighing 10 kgs!), which sent sound through a cable connecting it, like an umbilical cord, to the U-matic recorder.

I decided that Rachel was an obvious future sound recordist, and I remember spending more time teaching her sound than any of the others, diligently tutoring her in the craft of boom swinging and the dark art of microphone placement. She was very polite about it. Retrospectively, I think I might be responsible for her subsequent career choice and success as a producer and director!

One day, John Whitteron took a group of trainees out of town to shoot the sunrise. When they returned we gathered to watch what they had filmed. I remember being struck by how beautiful Warwick had made the sunrise look on ¾-inch video and I remember there was much praise for his work. He was a tall, skinny, shy and slightly awkward kid at the time, but on that day he was the hero. I don't want to romanticise the occasion too much but when I heard years later that he was doing cinematography at the AFTRS (Australian Film, Television and Radio School) I was not at all surprised.

The other highlight of that trip was discovering the amazing music that was being recorded by Indigenous artists at CAAMA radio. They were on sale as cassettes in the CAAMA shop. I loved bands like the Wedgetail Eagle

Band, Areyonga Desert Tigers and Ilkari Maru, and bought as many cassettes as possible. I had no idea that many years later I would rediscover them all over again while working with Warwick on the sound for his films *Green Bush* and *Samson & Delilah*.

Erica told me that Freda auditioned for the lead role in Charles Chauvel's *Jedda* (the part went to Rosalie Kunoth-Monks). This intrigued me because not long after I had been at CAAMA I was the sound recordist on Tracey Moffat's *Night Cries: A Rural Tragedy*, an imagined sequel to *Jedda*. Professor Marcia Langton played the role of an older, grown-up Jedda.

Beck Cole once said that seeing *Night Cries* was what made her pursue a career as a film director. She went on to collaborate with Warwick on many projects, later casting Professor Langton in her feature film *Here I Am*, on which Warwick was the director of photography and I was the sound designer.

The producer of *Night Cries* was Penny McDonald, who later became Warwick's partner. They had two children together, Rona and Dylan. I remember seeing Penny when she was pregnant with Dylan but it never crossed my mind that 20 years later I would be working as the sound designer, with Dylan as my director and

Penny as producer on the amazing documentary *Buckskin*.

Warwick and I were brought back together in the early 2000s when producer Kath Shelper asked me to be the sound designer on Warwick's short film *Green Bush*, and Beck Cole's film *Plains Empty*. Both films had been invited to the Sundance Film Festival and they needed to be finished on a tight schedule that went over Christmas and New Year. Beck and Warwick brought their daughter Luka May, who was only a baby, to the sound studio for the duration and I remember it as an intense, creative happy experience full of summer sun. I continued to work with Warwick as his sound designer during a period of success for him, with *Green Bush*, *Nana*, and *Samson & Delilah* all winning awards around the world.

Samson & Delilah is almost ten years old now but it still resonates with people. It got under the skin of the national psyche. It affected people in ways that they never expected. It changed the way people think. As a film, it is greater than the sum of it parts. I have sound designer credits on 40 feature films and have been the sound designer on 16 feature films since *Samson & Delilah*, but it is still the one people want to talk with me about the most!

I am sure there are many who have worked with Warwick, who would agree that the highest compliment he gives is 'That's gorgeous!'. When he says that to me I know my work has touched him.

There are lots of stories I can tell about *Samson & Delilah* but one comes to mind now because it also involves Erica. She would know that I couldn't possibly write this piece without recounting it!

We were having a screening to investors etc. on the final day of our final sound mix. In attendance were producer John Maynard and funding body representatives including Miranda Dear, Sally Riley and Erica Glynn (who was, at the time, head of the Indigenous unit at Screen Australia, I think). Warwick addressed the gathering, saying he was very proud of the film and didn't want to change a thing. This is a speech I've heard him make many times. I think one of Warwick's strengths is he knows instinctively when something is right. He just knows when the story has been told, through picture or sound, and when to embellish, or not to embellish, further. He trusts his creative collaborators but when he is happy with the result he knows when to stop.

After the screening, when the lights came on, Erica looked around the room and demanded to know why the soundtrack was filled with 'all those bloody New South Wales birds!'.

Warwick and I had carefully considered the birds

heard in the film. We had developed a totemic motif with Australian ravens and sulphur-crested cockatoos for the characters of *Samson & Delilah*. We had also used the sounds of topknot pigeons because Warwick loved the distinctive cooing sound they made. Erica was right though; many were from New South Wales, although they did cross the border into Central Australia. I stayed fairly quiet but it was great to see Warwick mount a defence as the two siblings 'debated' the provenance of the wildlife in the film!

I am now always rigorous about only using bird calls that would be heard in the locations depicted in the films I work on, and I research it carefully. Thank you, Erica!

It's comforting for me to know that once Warwick has decided something in the soundtrack works, he will defend it vigorously. Following his 'I'm very proud of this film and I don't want to change a thing' speech he has subsequently defended decisions we made with the sound for *True Gods* and *Big World* (his contributions to the film anthologies *Words With Gods* and *The Turning*, respectively).

Both Warwick and Erica have opened my ears to new sounds that I didn't even realise existed. They have both asked me, at different times, on different films they have directed, and without reference to each other, to put in the sound of a plane passing 35,000 feet (approximately10 kilometres) overhead. Living and working in Alice Springs, this is a sound they are familiar with, but I have never lived in a place where this sort of sound is heard and would never think to put it into a film. It's a sound that is only heard in extremely quiet places under a flight path (like Alice Springs), where the ambient noise level all around is so low that you can actually hear something 10 kilometres away. Warwick described it to me, and we put it in *Samson & Delilah*, heightening the scenes it is used in by adding it as an emotional texture at strategic points in the film.

Erica also asked me to put this sound in her beautiful, sad, inspiring film *Truth Be Told*, about the Indigenous soldiers who fought in the battle of Beersheba in World War I.

In this context the sound of the distant plane passing was used as a metaphor physically linking Australia and Israel, but also connecting the past to the present through distant memories.

Luckily the Glynn family likes cats because I have four of them (and up to seven at one point)! At various times Erica, Tanith, Dylan and Warwick have shared space with them while working with me at home. Harlequin went missing during the sound edit for *Samson & Delilah* and I don't think Warwick even thought twice about letting me take off a week to find him. Harlequin is now safely back home and

I remember Dylan was keen to meet him the first time he came to my house, such was the build up he was given by Warwick! Warwick still asks about Harlequin and likes to tell stories about The Darkness, his deaf white cat back in Alice Springs. He was insistent that the soundtrack of *Samson & Delilah* contained some sounds made by Milky, his Chihuahua, and if you listen carefully Milky can be heard barking in the background with the other community dogs in the first half of the film!

There are times when I'm working with Dylan, and he's sitting behind me, I can swear that the voice I'm hearing is Warwick's. Not so much the words he speaks but the sound of his voice, the timbre and the pitch. It's uncanny! But Dylan has his own voice and his own stories to tell.

From biographical films like *Buckskin*, which tells the story of Jack Buckskin, who is trying to revive the Aboriginal language of his ancestors in South Australia, or *Finding Maawirrangga*, about the redemption of the late Tom E. Lewis, to the humorous but achingly tragic *Nulla Nulla*, or his 'modern dreamtime' interpretation of the story of the emu and the kangaroo in *Coat of Arms*, Dylan is trying to tell important stories while always keeping his audience entertained.

Dylan is an impressive musician and composes the music

for most of his films himself. This allows my collaborations with him to grow organically as we work together to create a soundtrack where music and sound design merge to convey pure emotion at times.

I should mention at this point that he and his sister Rona performed the music for what I think is the greatest music cue ever composed for an Australian film. I'm referring to the cue *S4D Sad Song*, from *Samson & Delilah*, when Samson is banished from his community. Dylan's sparse electric guitar and Rona's delicate and brittle violin combine to make the hairs stand up on the back of my neck. Every time!

I'm so excited to see what Dylan does in the future. Having worked with him on four short films and two documentaries, I can say with certainty that he will be an important contributor to the Australian cultural conversation in coming years.

The first words I ever heard Tanith Glynn-Maloney speak were, 'What the fuck are you looking at!' Sadly for my story, these were not the words of Tanith but, rather, Jody, the character she played in Beck Cole's beautiful, way-before-its-time feature film, *Here I Am*, about an Indigenous women's halfway house. There's definitely a hint of Jody in Tanith but without the world-weariness – and with a much better sense of humour!

I've worked with Tanith as producer on numerous films directed by Dylan. It's exciting to watch a new generation of the Glynn family, who weren't even born when I met Freda, Warwick and Erica, tell their stories with a fresh original voice. This includes Warwick and Beck's now almost grown-up daughter, Luka May Glynn-Cole, who is starting to make her mark as an actor.

In recent years it has been so good to see Freda as the mother and nana, at screenings or after parties for films made by her children or grandchildren, a proud matriarch enjoying their success!

As a sound guy, I spend a lot of time with clients behind me while I work on the sound. The nature of my job means a lot of time is spent listening to sounds, and while they are playing there is no room for talking. I realise that I have spent literally hundreds, perhaps thousands, of hours with Warwick, Erica, Dylan and Tanith sitting behind me, none of us speaking, just absorbed by sound and image. I can honestly say that at these times I've often felt my most creative and most content.

In 2009, **David Jowsey** formed Bunya Productions with award-winning filmmaker Ivan Sen. Bunya is a boutique feature production company based out of Sydney and Brisbane. David has produced a slate of award-winning feature films including *Mad Bastards, Toomelah, Satellite Boy* as well as *Mystery Road, Goldstone, Jasper Jones* and *Sweet Country* with Greer Simpkin. With Simpkin David Jowsey most recently produced the TV drama *Mystery Road – The Series* for ABC TV.

the backyard

David Jowsey

'I'm not your bloody aunty,' Erica Glynn tells a circle of friends and family in her backyard. Erica is telling us about a young Aboriginal guy who called her 'Aunty'. She says, 'I'm too young to be called Aunty' – and nobody disagrees.

Erica ran Screen Australia's Indigenous Department for about 11 years and made a fantastic contribution to Aboriginal media development. Her spare but perceptive comments about script, whether for the shortest short or a feature, were always offered with a generous and collaborative spirit, designed to improve the script.

On the other end of the process, her input to cuts in postproduction was also always valuable. She wouldn't say too much but what she did say was big picture articulation of an issue in the cut or an enhancement that could be made. This is the stuff a filmmaking team really needs. It's not uncommon for an inexperienced or first-time director to be resistant to input, usually due to underlying anxiety or confidence, or both. It's a big deal when the boss from Screen Australia comes to your edit suite and you have to present the work to the world for the first time. Erica, as a filmmaker herself, brings an awareness of that stress and doesn't bring any ego-driven comments to the work; she just really understands storytelling.

I believe Erica, with her passion, strength and straight talking delivered on dozens of projects over many years, deserves more credit for her part in the development and creation of the Indigenous film and television sector.

At the backyard gathering at Erica's, Warwick has cooked up a full-scale gourmet meal for everyone gathered. It is often said that someone or other is a good cook, but Warwick is at another level. He hasn't trained as a chef or worked in the hospitality industry but he spends a chunk of his spare time watching cooking shows and that's how he researches cooking techniques. Those who have experienced his culinary prowess have often said to him, 'You should do a cooking show, Wok' and apparently he might be finally ready to do that. You can just imagine Warwick in his TV kitchen, armed with his wit and his one-liners, biting at the plump gusset of Australian comfort.

Even if the meal is being served in the backyard, it's presented with style. Warwick is a thoughtful bloke and generous soul. He has considered the vegetarians and the meat eaters. Freda is visiting from Queensland and pops outside to say hi to everyone in the backyard. She quietly slips around probing each person's wellbeing with that sort of intimacy special people possess; when she talks to you, she makes you feel like you're the only person in the room.

I reckon Freda, with her fierce intelligence, has always seen into people and been very perceptive about them. I'm sure this is a defensive trait from her years of fighting the system, both as a young woman and as a leader in the fight for Indigenous media rights and access. Her perceptiveness worked to her advantage when, in her regional Queensland home, she experienced a neighbour acting crazy, in fact scary crazy, and she felt so worried by it she left her property. A short while later the neighbour murdered one of the locals. If she had stayed, it very likely would have been Freda.

As night falls in the backyard, its time to light the fire, the fire pit is made from the stainless-steel innards of an old washing machine – perfect for a communal fire, with its dozens of little holes letting the heat out onto your legs.

The mob gather round the fire and stories soon turn to discussion about film, the films we have worked on now and earlier. There's plenty of talk about *Sweet Country*. David Tranter is a bloody sound recordist who doesn't write much, so how in the hell did he come up with such a terrific screenplay? Well it's his family story and it's a true history. He actually hand drew the whole yarn. I love turning the pages of his blue-pen drawings with snatches of dialogue, it's simply an amazing genesis of *Sweet Country*. Warwick and Dave grew up together since they were little boys in Alice Springs so to shoot the story there in the sublimely beautiful mountains was a wonderful thing.

Warwick is a happy filmmaker with friends and family around him in the backyard with the fire lighting the night and drinks or whatever you want available to share. Freda heads to bed, Erica not long after, but Warwick stays up late, as usual.

This story of mine seems to be about the simple things in life – great food, wine and song shared with friends and family, stories and laughter rolling long into the night around the fire. Actually that's not what it is about – it's really about talent, simple, rare-as-hen's-teeth talent.

Erica and Warwick have it and that's why they make such great films – they are special and rare and deserve all the accolades, because they are very talented filmmakers. 'It's talent. Either you got it or you ain't,' said Mel Brooks.

Faye Ginsburg

is director of the Center for Media, Culture and History at New York University and has been writing on, teaching about, programming, and an advocate for Indigenous media in Australia, New Zealand/Aotearoa and across the Americas since 1988, when she first met Freda Glynn in Alice Springs. An author/editor of four books, she is also the Kriser Professor of Anthropology at NYU, and director of the Center for Disability Studies. She is currently completing a very overdue book, *Mediating Culture: Indigenous Media in a Digital Age*.

a fan letter from the Big Apple

Faye Ginsburg

Sitting on my desk is one of my favorite photographs, the one that reminds me of the privilege of meeting Freda Glynn for the first time, a visual record of a door-opening moment in July of 1988. As a new professor at NYU, I was trying to decolonise the teaching of documentary in my classes. I had heard about the Central Australian Aboriginal Media Association (CAAMA) from Fred Myers, my colleague at New York University (NYU) who had been working in Central Australia with Pintupi people since the 1970s; we had recently married. Eager to learn about CAAMA firsthand, I went to Alice Springs with Fred, and phoned CAAMA to ask for an interview with Freda; she graciously granted time to me, a stranger from NYC.

Thanks to that first meeting with Freda and eventually with her equally talented progeny, I have been a huge fan of Aboriginal and Torres Strait Islander media and the people who make this work, writing about it, programming, and promoting this work for three decades.

Faye Ginsburg (right) with Freda in Alice Springs, 1988
(Photo: Fred Myers)

Looking at the photo taken at that first encounter, you can sense the crisp air of an Alice Springs winter day. Freda and I are sitting outside on chairs carefully positioned to catch the sun in front of one of the temporary units that housed CAAMA in its location at the time, at the Little Sisters town camp. Dressed in a light-grey cotton sweater, jeans and tall brown boots, her dark hair falling just over her ears in a no-nonsense bob, Freda's hand is poised in the air for emphasis. She is looking intently at me to be sure I am catching everything, while she relates the intertwined histories of CAAMA's birth and her remarkable life as an Indigenous cultural activist. I remember being absolutely bowled over by Freda's creativity, grit, generosity and imagination, all woven into her work with CAAMA.

The year before the photo was taken, CAAMA had won a David vs. Goliath fight for the licence to the satellite broadcast rights for Central Australia, what became Imparja TV. It went to air in 1988; by the time I was talking to her in July, Freda was the only female chair of a television network in the world. I remember how impressed I was to learn that CAAMA was crucial in providing Indigenous television in Central Australian languages, produced by Indigenous directors, and broadcast to remote Aboriginal communities. Two shows were notable in carrying out this mission: *Nganampa Anwernekenhe* ('ours' in Pitjantjatjara and Arrernte languages) and *Urrpeye* (Messenger); many accomplished next generation First Nations filmmakers, including Freda's children Erica Glynn and Warwick Thornton, first began their work as media makers on these shows.

During the years after that first meeting with Freda, I wrote and taught extensively on Indigenous Australian media, bringing many Indigenous Australian filmmakers to NYC to show and talk about their work. In 2009, I was asked to help with film programming to accompany a show of early Aboriginal paintings from Papunya at NYU's Grey Art Gallery. Fred Myers helped arrange that show, concerned that NYC audiences understand the contemporary range of Indigenous arts beyond the well-known dot paintings associated with Papunya Tula. That same year, Freda's son Warwick – who had cut his teeth first as a DJ at CAAMA radio and made his first films there as well – completed his inaugural feature film, *Samson & Delilah* (2009). The film walked away with the Camera d'Or for best first feature at the prestigious Cannes Film Festival, while picking up 14 awards at many other festivals; Indigenous painting in Central Australia is an important subplot to the central story of the intertwined and complex lives of two Aboriginal teens. Warwick was headed to the US for a screening of the film at the Brooklyn Academy of Music. I arranged a screening at the Museum of Modern Art (MoMA) associated with the show. As a host for Warwick and producer Kath Shelper on this NYC trip, I was thrilled to get to know how Freda's remarkable son was carrying on her mission, bringing his own extraordinary talent to Indigenous storytelling, moving from the formats of radio and television to developing a new wave of cinematic work that was taking its place on the world stage. Among the places he first wanted to visit in the Big Apple? Matt Umanov's legendary guitar store.

On a trip to Australia in 2010, I had the chance to meet Erica Glynn, Freda's daughter – also a notable filmmaker of films I had long admired, such as *My Bed Your Bed*; *Agnes, Maude & Pearly Too*; and *Ngangkari*. Erica was serving as head of Indigenous work at Screen Australia. There, she carried on Freda's legacy by making new opportunities available for emerging and established Aboriginal filmmakers, in both urban and remote settings, taking Indigenous television to new heights as the executive producer of the path-breaking series *Redfern Now, The Gods of Wheat Street*, and *8MMM Aboriginal Radio*, the last an hilarious homage to and send-up of CAAMA radio and life in Alice Springs. Erica returned to full-time filmmaking in 2014, directing the much-loved *Black Comedy* series in 2016, and her very moving documentary on Indigenous literacy, *In My Own Words*, in 2017. Erica and I corresponded regularly about showing new Indigenous Australian work in NYC festivals. The last exchange we had before Erica left Screen Australia, was about bringing Dylan McDonald (now Dylan River) for a US premiere of his very moving 2014 documentary

Buckskin at the Margaret Mead Film Festival, where we were also planning to have a NYC premiere of *The Darkside* with Dylan's father Warwick; a chance to showcase both the father–son team and the Glynn legacy. Both made it to NYC from Toronto after screening work at *imagine*NATIVE *Film + Media Arts Festival* (a partner with the Mead festival), the major international Indigenous film festival held every October in Canada, and where Warwick received their Milestone Award in 2014.

When I wrote to Screen Australia in 2016 to see if we could bring *Songlines on Screen* to the Mead Festival, I recognised a new name in the email reply: Tanith Glynn-Maloney. I remembered seeing her as Jodi in Beck Cole's feature, *Here I Am* (2011) and her name appeared as producer on *Nulla Nulla* (2015). Not only did Tanith help bring the *Songlines* work to NYC, she also recommended a new short film from CAAMA, by a first-time filmmaker Viviana Petyarre, which was a wonderful addition to the festival line-up. Multi-talented as an actor and producer, promoter of Indigenous work at Screen Australia, with roots in CAAMA, and founder of Since 1788 Productions, it was clear that Tanith was part of the Glynn-eage.

In 2017, while on tour with his stunning and enormously successful feature film *Sweet Country*, Warwick came back to NYC once again to the Margaret Mead Film Festival, this time for a premiere of his cheeky and deadly serious experimental documentary, *We Don't Need a Map*. It won the 2017 Margaret Mead Filmmaker Award the same night that *Sweet Country* won the Best Dramatic Feature Award at imagineNATIVE in Toronto.

I am sure there will be more stories to tell of the legacy of the Glynn-eage, that now has a recognised place in the Big Apple. I am so profoundly grateful to Freda for welcoming me into her orbit back in 1988, and for the work she has done to decolonise Indigenous representation, keeping the stories (and languages) of remote Indigenous lives vividly present. Her work clearly inspired new generations of Glynn family cultural activists and filmmakers, all nurtured on the principles and practices that Freda first established. They are adding their voices and visions to the project she launched, honouring the past as they walk into the future, and reminding us all why Indigenous lives matter.

Mary-Ellen Mullane

is senior commissioning editor at NITV. Her recent commissions include the award-winning *You Are Here* slate of landmark documentaries, working with Indigenous filmmakers including Warwick Thornton, Erica Glynn, Darren Dale, Dean Gibson, Tyson Mowarin and Trish Morton-Thomas among others. She also commissioned NITV's Logie Award winning children's animation series *Little J & Big Cuz* and the live action series *Grace Beside Me*.

do better

Mary-Ellen Mullane

It's a wild ride, the Australian film industry; full of fortune hunters and gamblers and fakes, drawn to it like moths to a flame. We all have a touch of the kamikaze about us. Erica has some of the above, minus the fake bit. There is nothing fake about Erica. She is the real deal.

I met Erica about 10 years ago when I went to work at Screen Australia and I was a bit scared of her. Erica worked in the Indigenous Unit and she was the moral compass of the place. It wasn't a chosen role, she had it forced on her. The Indigenous Unit was at the centre, and the rest of the organisation revolved around it. Erica infused all her work with meaning and purpose, and during that time *Samson & Delilah, The Sapphires, Redfern Now, Satellite Boy, The Gods of Wheat Street, Here I Am, Coniston* – just to name a few – were born. It was a very exciting time in the Australian film industry, largely thanks to people like Erica. She introduced Australia to a whole new raft of Indigenous writing, directing and producing talent, all the while holding the line, no matter how much more complicated or difficult it made her work and life. Erica earnt the equivalent of a PhD in filmmaking ethics over the course of those years and was there to teach anyone willing to listen, both black and white. One day, at a farewell morning tea, a clerk from the finance department said to Erica, 'I am from Mt Gambier in South Australia but I had to come here to Screen Australia in Woolloomooloo to meet an Aboriginal person. I'm so ashamed that I was so ignorant for so long.' As is the case for many women in the Australian film and television industry, Erica was helping a large number of others, like this clerk, and right on up to international feature film producers, while putting her own career as a filmmaker on hold in the process.

Another time, a cold, rainy Saturday afternoon during the Sydney Film Festival, I saw Erica have an out-of-body experience after a screening of the American indie feature film *Beasts of The Southern Wild.* She loved that film. She loved the ideas in it. She is a vacuum-upper of ideas. It's the idea that drives her, I realised standing in the queue at Event Cinemas in George Street, Sydney. Is that her gift or just plain raw talent shining through? Erica can gossip, give advice, talk books, art and theatre all at once, as long as there is a good solid idea to yarn about, she is happy.

Fast forward 10 years and, in many ways sadly, not enough has changed. Many of the benchmarks achieved by Erica back then still stand. What was new and fresh has become the established and, a decade on, her people still struggle, in some ways more so. As I write this Pat Dodson is calling for urgent reforms to the justice system, his voice breaking in sheer frustration. He's asking bureaucrats to spend their Easter coming up with a solution to the soaring rates of incarceration of Aboriginal and Torres Strait Islander peoples. We can solve this problem with enough imagination, he says, we can do better!

And Erica knows a lot about imagination. Not long after I started at National Indigenous Television (NITV) I ran into Erica in Alice Springs where she was writing a television series set in a fictional Aboriginal community located in the breathtakingly beautiful McDonald Ranges, around 150 km west of Alice Springs. Her eyes were sparkling; she was enjoying herself, up to her elbows in story and plot. She was free from Screen Australia's responsibilities and back in the film and television production sector, working on her own projects. And she was doing her bit of heavy lifting for Pat; she was using her imagination to conjure up contemporary Arrente experience and make it part of the nation's consciousness. It's harder to turn away from people who are seen and heard in all their complexity and humanity.

A small but perfect oeuvre of work, her films are quiet, personal and deeply political. Her recent films made for NITV, *In My Own Words* and *Truth Be Told*, punch above their weight. Invited to screen at film festivals, they are also destined for parliamentary screenings where politicians are shamed and contrite. So how long does it have to go on, this showing and telling? Erica is impatient and frustrated with the world of politics and, at times, filmmaking too. Regardless, she is tender and kind to those who most need it. In the small town of Brewarrina, in northwest NSW, she is a legend. In 2016 she spent nine months in Bre making a film *with* the community, not *about* or *on* the community. And her film is true and heartbreaking and funny and loved by its subjects and audiences alike. Above all, it is compassionate. Erica fell in love with the people in her film and they fell in love with her right back. You can see it on screen. I am in awe of Erica's ability to love, and how it is perfectly balanced with her ability to fight. She knows a lot more about the complexities of love than most people. With people like Erica in our world, we all do what we do, better.

a haiku

for warwick wok wallis

---

von schtoop

gifted wounded child
drunken nuisance, kind as fuck
poetic prophet

with thanks

Amanda Duthie

Creative Director/CEO, Adelaide Film Festival

The notion of this book to mark the extraordinary legacy of Freda Glynn came to me on the red carpet at the Venice Film Festival. The music of Johnny Cash was playing as I watched Warwick and Dylan, father and son, saunter through the Italian sunlight. Very rock'n'roll. We were walking into a cinema for the world premiere of *Sweet Country*, about to experience an international audience's response to this incredible film. It ended with a standing ovation.

Family. Kin. Dynasty.

What is the difference? Family combines the love and fun and troubles that beset us – as parents, as children, the nuclear family and beyond.

Dynasty is when you see the generations of a family from afar – the work, the passion and the truth that they create as a shape in the world.

The Glynn family does all that.

This collection is more than screen stories – it is about the ties that bind and the ties that draw us closer. So much good work created.

It has been a privilege to gather these tales into one bound edition from people who bear witness to the work of these three generations. Of course there are many many more people who contributed to building CAAMA and supported the careers and the slate of work produced by these extraordinary filmmakers. The contributions in *Kin* go some way to pulling together these stories. It's a subject and a history that needs to be told.

Warm thanks to Anna Zagala for her work on *Kin*.

Thanks to Freda, Erica and Tanith and Dylan and Warwick for your screen storytelling.

But mostly I send thanks to all the mothers and aunties who have created so much in our community but are not known – or not known well enough. This is for you.

filmography

Erica Glynn

Director

2018 *She Who Must Be Loved* (documentary)
Truth Be Told: Lest We Forget (documentary)

2017 *In My Own Words* (documentary)

2016 *Black Comedy* (series)

2006 *Knot at Home Project* (documentary series)

2001 *Ngangkari* (documentary)

1999 *Agnes, Maude & Pearly Too* (short)

1998 *My Bed Your Bed* (short)

Executive Producer

2015 8MMM Aboriginal Radio (series – 6 episodes)
Redfern Now: Promise Me (telefeature)

2014 *The Gods of Wheat Street* (series – 6 episodes)

2012–13 *Redfern Now* (series – 12 episodes)

2005 *Endangered* (documentary)

Writer

2017 *Little J & Big Cuz* (TV series, 2 episodes: *Where's Aaron? Goanna Ate My Homework*)
In My Own Words (Documentary)

2001 *Ngangkari* (short documentary, concept)

Warwick Thornton

Director

2017	*Sweet Country*
	We Don't Need a Map (documentary)
2015	*The Way of the Ngangkari* (video installation)
2014	'True Gods' (within *Words with Gods*, feature)
2013	*The Darkside*
	'Big World' (within *The Turning*, feature)
2011	*Stranded* (video installation)
2010	*Art+Soul* (documentary series)
2009	*Samson & Delilah*
2007	*Nana* (short)
2005	*The Old Man and the Inland Sea* (documentary)
	Green Bush (short)
2002	*Mimi* (short)
1996	*From Sand to Celluloid: Payback* (short)

Cinematographer

2017	*Sweet Country*
	Coat of Arms (short)
	We Don't Need a Map (documentary)
2015	*The Way of the Ngangkari* (moving image)
	Septembers of Shiraz
	Black Chook (short)
2014	'True Gods' (within *Words with Gods*, feature)

2013	*The Darkside*
	'Big World' (within *The Turning*, feature)
2012	*The Oysterman* (short)
	In the Air (short)
	The Sapphires
2011	*Here I Am*
	Stranded (moving image)
2010	*Art+Soul* (documentary series, 3 episodes)
	Karlu Karlu: Devil's Marbles (TV, short documentary)
2009	*Samson & Delilah*
2008	*Keao* (short)
	First Australians (documentary series)
	Bit of Black Business
2006	*My Brother Vinnie* (short)
	Knot at Home Project (documentary)
2005	*The Old Man and the Inland Sea* (documentary)
	5 Seasons (documentary)
	Plains Empty (short)
2004	*Beyond Sorry* (documentary)
	Flat (short)
2002	*Jabiru 0886: Trespass* (documentary)
	Mimi (short)
2001	*Ngangkari* (documentary)

	My Mother India (documentary)
2000	*Buried Country* (documentary)
1999	*Stone Forever* (documentary)
1998	*Radiance*

Writer

2017	*We Don't Need a Map* (documentary)
2013	'Big World' (within *The Turning*, feature)
2009	*Samson & Delilah*
2007	*Nana* (short)
2005	*The Old Man and the Inland Sea* (documentary)
	Green Bush (short)
2002	Mimi (short)
1996	*From Sand to Celluloid: Payback* (short)

Dylan River

Director

2018	*Finke: There and Back* (documentary)
2017	*Coat of Arms* (short)
	Finding Maawirrangga (documentary)
2015	*Black Chook* (short)
	Nulla Nulla (short)
2013	*Buckskin* (documentary)

Cinematographer

2017	*Carry the Flag* (documentary)
	Blasko (documentary)

	Sweet Country
	Finding Maawirrangga (documentary)
	We Don't Need a Map (documentary)
2016	*Static Wind* (short)
2015	*Ten Thousand* (short)
2014	*Who We Are: Brave New Clan* (documentary)
	Talking Language with Ernie Dingo (documentary)

Writer

2018	*Finke: There and Back* (documentary)
2017	*Coat of Arms* (short)
2016	*Black Comedy* (series – 1 episode)
2015	*Nulla Nulla* (short)

Composer

2015	*Nulla Nulla* (short)
2013	*Buckskin* (documentary)

Tanith Glynn-Maloney

Producer

2018	*She Who Must Be Loved* (documentary)
	Truth Be Told: Lest We Forget (documentary)
	Ward One (short)
2017	*Every King Tide* (VR documentary), co-producer
	Petyarre (documentary), co-producer
2015	*Nulla Nulla* (short)

Wakefield Press is an independent publishing and distribution company based in Adelaide, South Australia. We love good stories and publish beautiful books. To see our full range of books, please visit our website at www.wakefieldpress.com.au where all titles are available for purchase. To keep up with our latest releases, news and events, subscribe to our monthly newsletter.

Find us!

Facebook: www.facebook.com/wakefield.press
Twitter: www.twitter.com/wakefieldpress
Instagram: www.instagram.com/wakefieldpress

www.ingramcontent.com/pod-product-compliance
Ingram Content Group Australia Pty Ltd
76 Discovery Rd, Dandenong South VIC 3175, AU
AUHW010839111125
419315AU00010B/81

9 781743 056028